Please leave us a review!

Thank you for purchasing this resource.

We'd be thrilled if you
left us a review on the website
where you purchased this.

TABLE OF CONTENTS

2 · Introduction For Parents and Educators

3 · The Super Sleuths

CRITICAL THINKING EXERCISES

4 · Section 1: Spatial Reasoning

28 · Section 2: Identification

36 · Section 3: Patterns & Sequencing

50 · Section 4: Verbal Reasoning

62 · Section 5: Quantitative Reasoning

85 · Section 6: Logic Matrices

94 · Certificate of Completion

95 · Answer Key

INTRODUCTION
For Parents and Educators

Thank you for selecting this resource. Congratulations on helping your young scholar build vital critical thinking skills!

These exercises:

- build critical thinking ability
- improve logic analysis skills
- increase focus

Most exercises are relatively brief. Most do not require an advanced level of reading to complete.

These exercises differ from activities your child completes at school. Therefore, your child may need guidance in answering these initially.

Book Sections (Question Types)
- Spatial Reasoning

Book Sections, continued
- Identification
- Patterns & Sequencing
- Verbal Reasoning
- Quantitative Reasoning
- Logic Matrices

To increase engagement, a detective theme accompanies this resource (see the next page).

As your child completes each page of activities (pages 6-93), she/he earns one point.

If she/he completes all pages with questions, she/he becomes a detective with the Super Sleuth Detective Agency.

Don't forget the certificate on page 94!

THE SUPER SLEUTHS

We need your help!

The Super Sleuth detective agency needs another detective.

WE THINK YOU HAVE WHAT IT TAKES.

THE SUPER SLEUTHS

Ana   Max   Lee   Ben

To prove you have what it takes, you must first put your skills to the test using this book. It's filled with **mind-bending, challenging questions that only a Super Sleuth could answer.** For each page you finish, you'll earn one point. If you finish all the pages, you will have earned **77** points: enough to join the Super Sleuths!

I bet you'll give up!

←SLY

Watch out for this bad guy – Sly – the villain. He doesn't want any more Super Sleuths. The more Super Sleuths, the more detectives investigating his crimes. Sly doesn't think you can earn 77 points. He thinks you'll give up. However, we know you'll prove him wrong!

🔍 **REMEMBER,** for each page you finish, you'll earn one point.
🔍 Look for the pages with the boxes at the bottom. These are the pages you must finish. After finishing a page, check the box.

Think of a detective name for yourself.
When you're ready to start, **sign your detective name on the line below.**

ABOUT SPATIAL REASONING
for parents and educators

Spatial reasoning involves analyzing various aspects of an object, such as a shape or group of shapes.

Your child will analyze things like object:

- appearance (number of sides, design, etc.)
- quantity
- position (rotation, angle, etc.)
- relation to other objects

Developing this skill improves children's abilities in math and, naturally, in STEM.

Spatial reasoning is assessed on almost all gifted and talented admissions tests.

Spatial reasoning skills are developed in this section through:

- Classification
- Analogies
- Rotation Design
- Matching
- Replication

SECTION 1

SPATIAL REASONING

Sly, the villain, doesn't think you can do the questions because they're **tricky**.

HOWEVER, WE KNOW YOU CAN DO IT!

You won't give up, will you (even if it takes a few tries)?

Don't forget: after doing each page, check the box at the bottom:

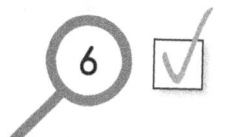

You earn 1 point for each page you do.

PICTURE PARTS

Match the group of pieces used to make the disguise with the assembled disguise on the bottom.

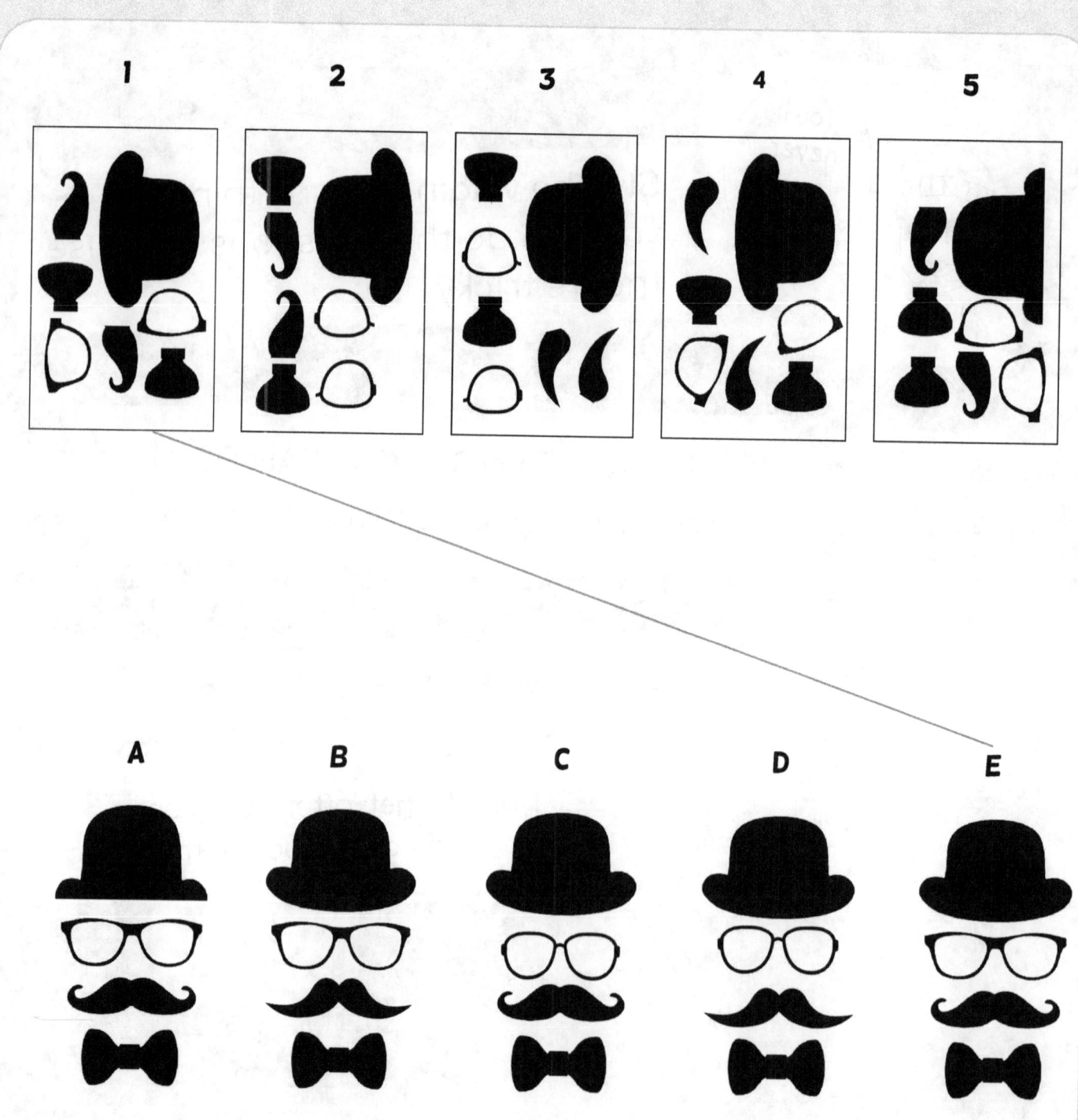

SPATIAL REASONING

SHAPE GROUPS

Match the picture on the left with the group of pieces that were used to make it on the right. (Remember that the shapes can rotate.)

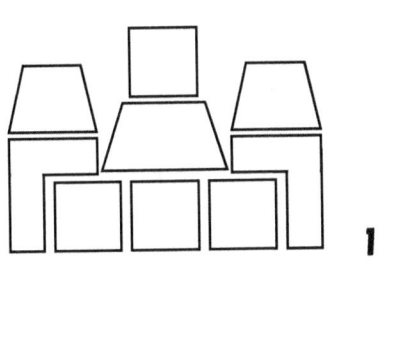

1

A

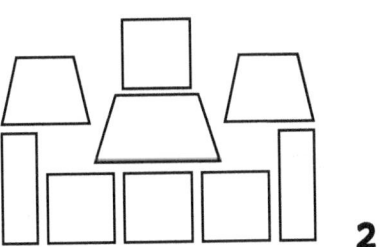

2

B

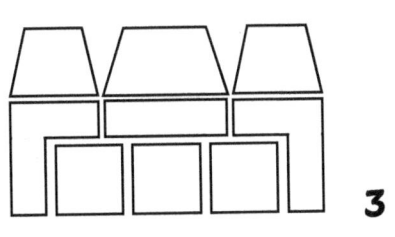

3

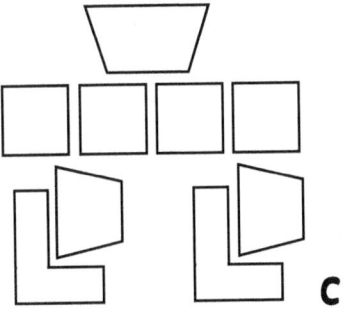

C

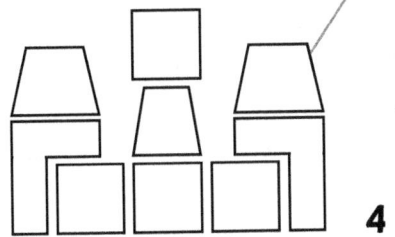

4

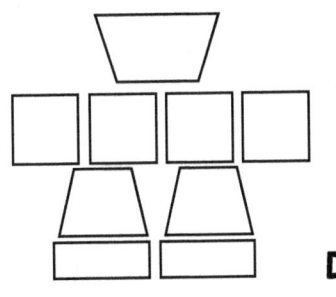

D

WHICH ONE DOES NOT BELONG?

These shapes are alike in some way, except for one shape. Can you figure out which shape does not belong?

Example: Let's figure out what each of the shapes (except one) have in common. They each have four sides. So, let's cross out the 6-sided shape (the hexagon).

(Parent note: The answer choices are not labelled A, B, C, etc. In the Answer Key, Choice 1 = A, Choice 2 = B, Choice 3 = C, Choice 4 = D, Choice 5 = E.)

1. EXAMPLE

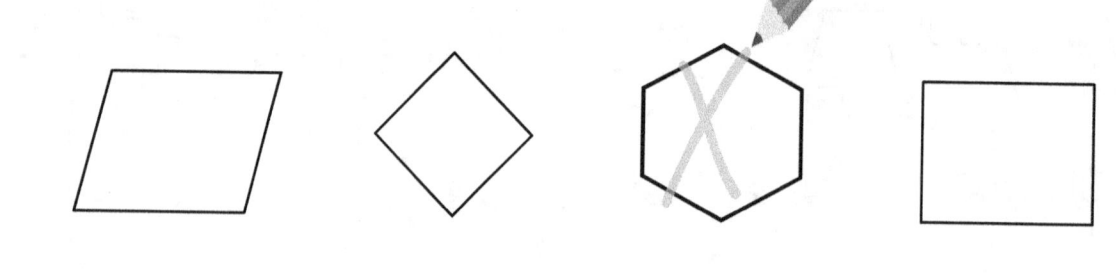

2.

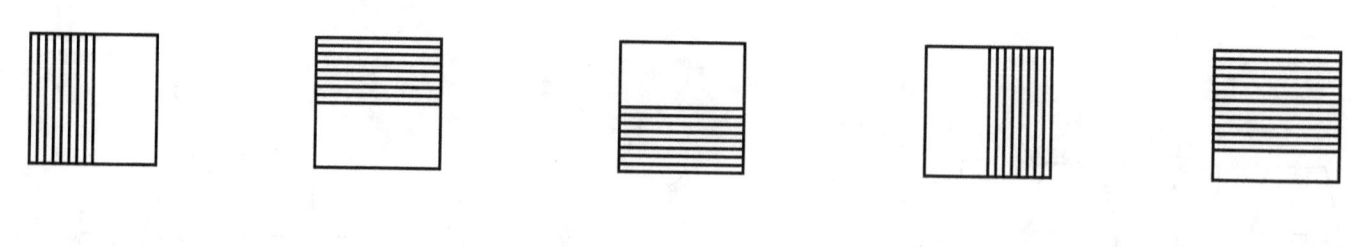

SPATIAL REASONING

WHICH ONE DOES NOT BELONG?

These shapes are alike in some way, except for one shape. Can you figure out which shape does not belong?

3.

 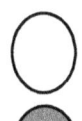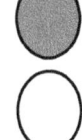 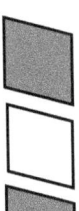  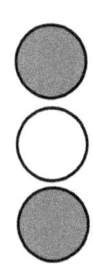

4.

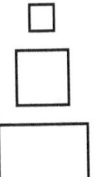   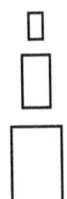 

WHICH ONE DOES NOT BELONG?

These shapes are alike in some way, except for one shape. Can you figure out which shape does not belong?

5.

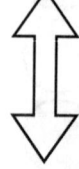 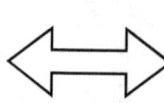   

6.

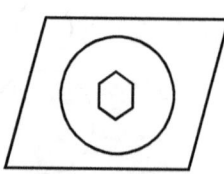 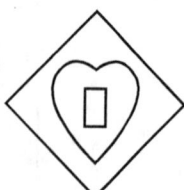   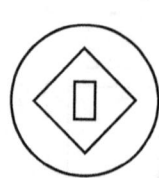

SPATIAL REASONING

WHICH ONE DOES NOT BELONG?

These shapes are alike in some way, except for one shape. Can you figure out which shape does not belong?

7.

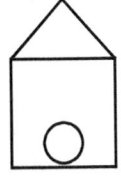  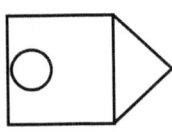 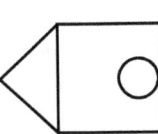 

8.

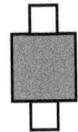 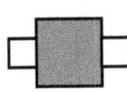 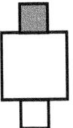 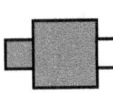 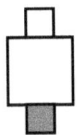

WHICH ONE DOES NOT BELONG?

These shapes are alike in some way, except for one shape. Can you figure out which shape does not belong?

9.

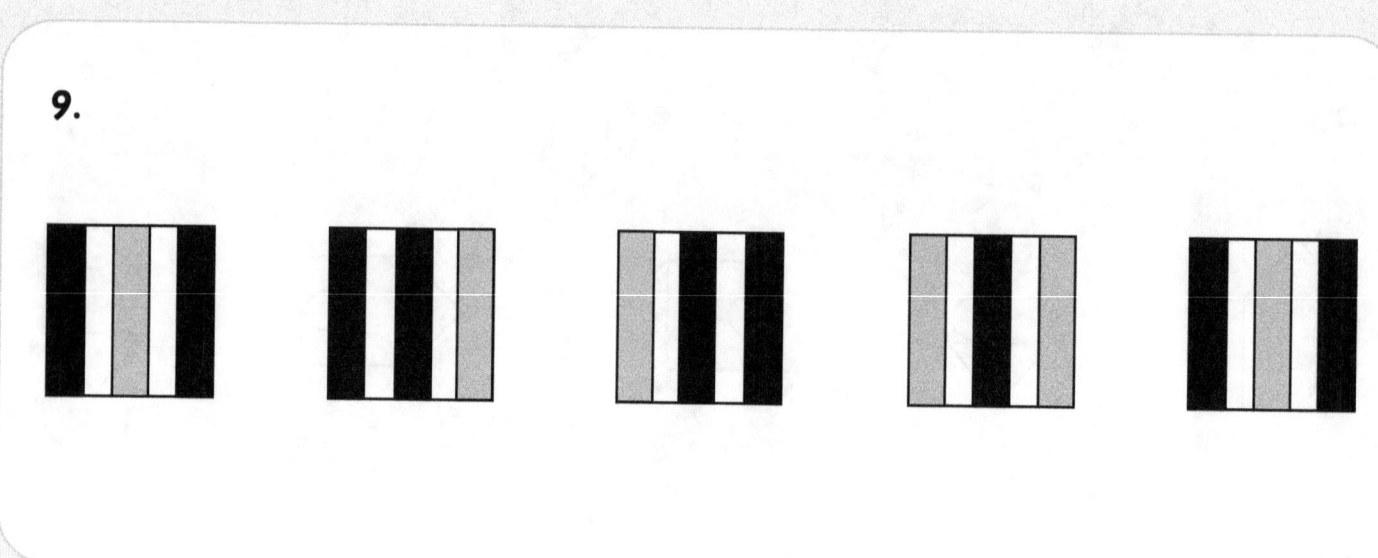

10.

SPATIAL REASONING

WHICH ONE DOES NOT BELONG?

These shapes are alike in some way, except for one shape. Can you figure out which shape does not belong?

11.

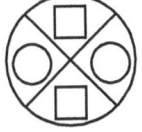    

12.

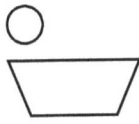 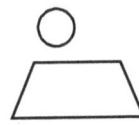  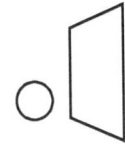 

WHAT COMES NEXT?

The shapes below are rotating. Look at the direction they are rotating ↻. Can you see how the dark part rotates? Color in the last 2 shapes to show how they would look as they rotate.

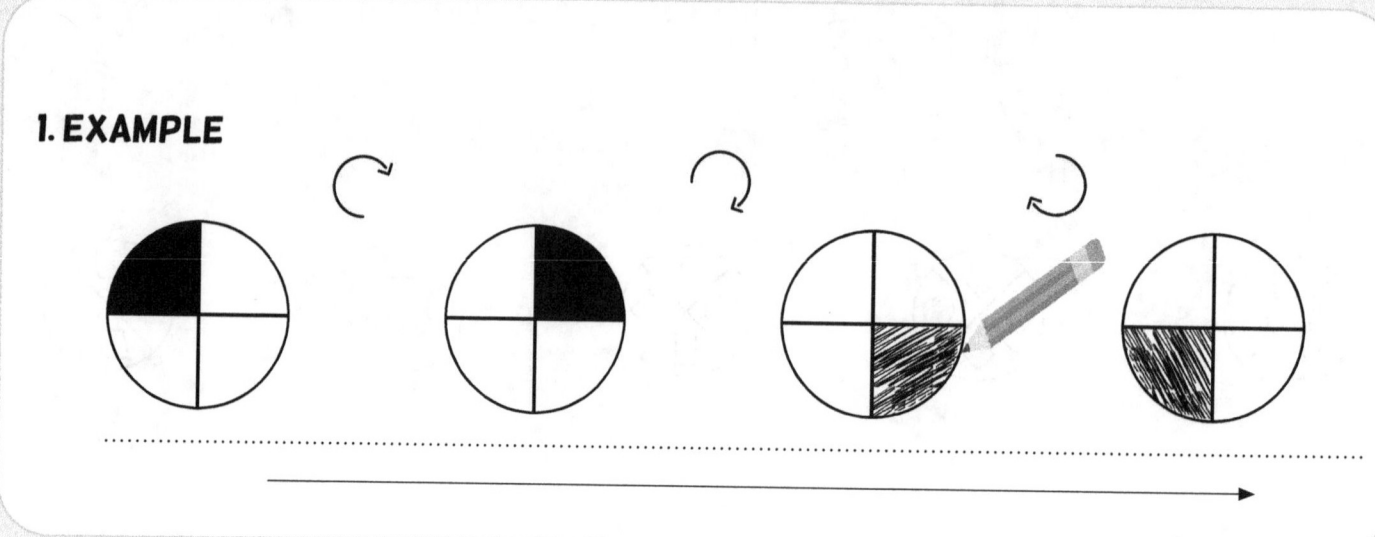

1. EXAMPLE

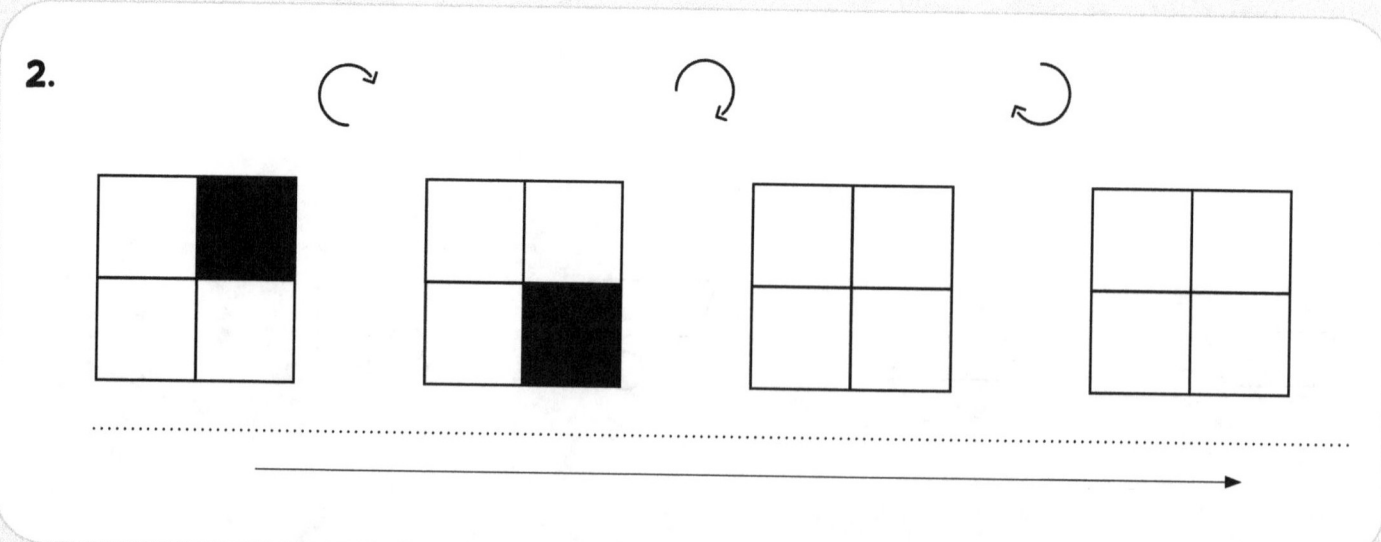

2.

SPATIAL REASONING

WHAT COMES NEXT?

The shapes below are rotating. Look at the direction they are rotating ↻. Can you see how the dark part rotates? Color in the last 2 shapes to show how they would look as they rotate.

3.

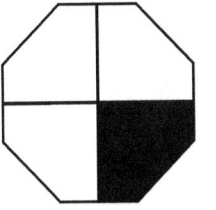 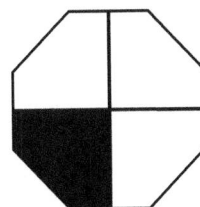 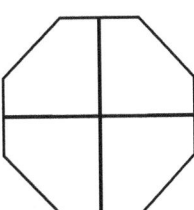 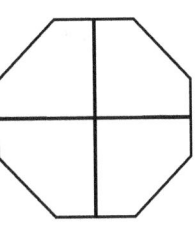

4.

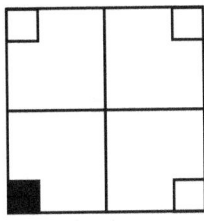 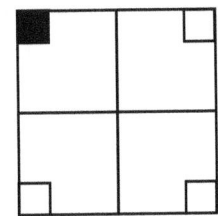 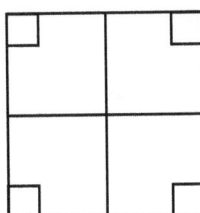 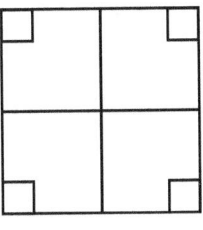

WHAT IS MISSING?

The top pictures go together in some way. Which picture would make the bottom pictures go together in the same way that the top pictures do? Circle your answer.

Example (#1): Look at the 2 pictures on top. In the first box we see one heart. In the second box are two hearts. Let's try to come up with a "rule" to describe how the pictures change from the first box to the second box. The rule would be: "add one." How would we use this rule with the picture in the bottom box? We see 1 diamond. If our rule is "add one," then 2 diamonds is the answer. (Parent note: The answer choices aren't labelled A, B, etc. In the Answer Key, Choice 1 = A, Choice 2 = B, Choice 3 = C, Choice 4 = D.)

1. EXAMPLE

2.

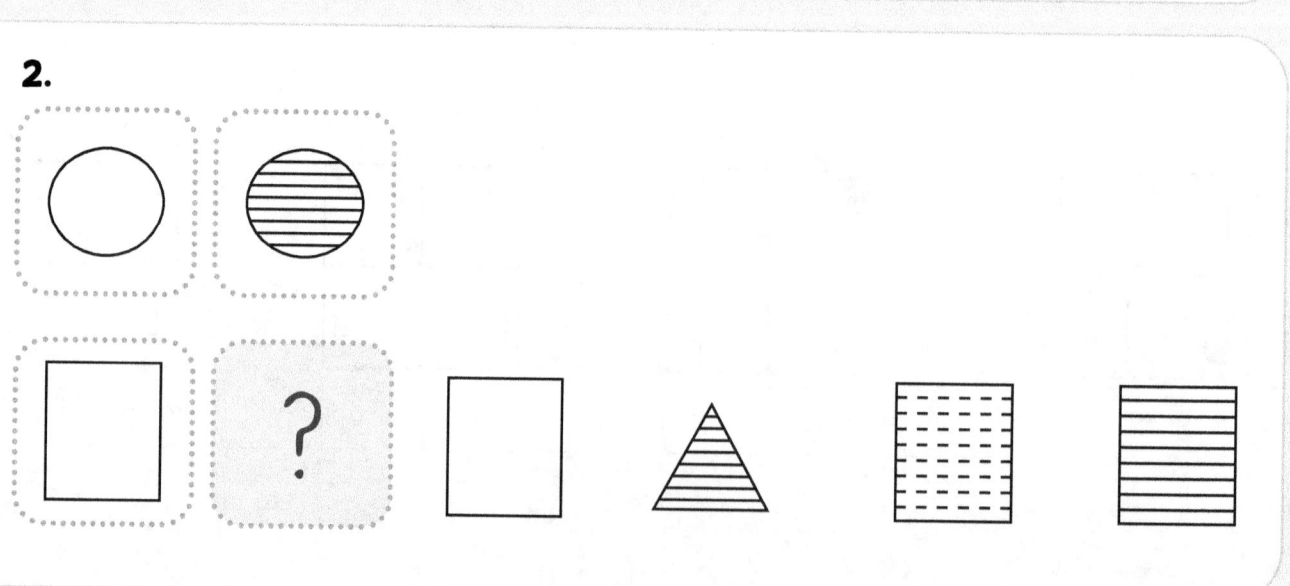

SPATIAL REASONING

WHAT IS MISSING?

The top pictures go together in some way. Which picture would make the bottom pictures go together in the same way that the top pictures do? Circle your answer.

3.

4.

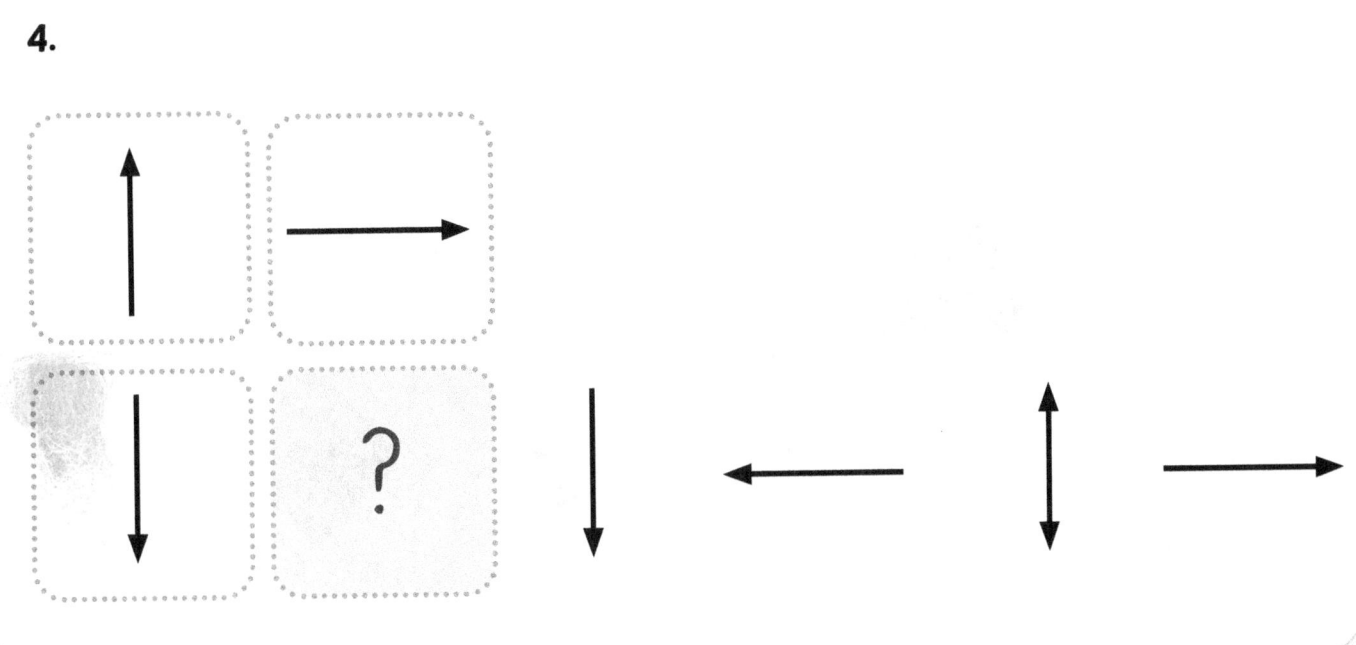

WHAT IS MISSING?

The top pictures go together in some way. Which picture would make the bottom pictures go together in the same way that the top pictures do? Circle your answer.

5.

    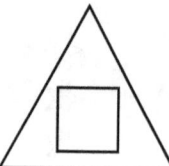

6.

SPATIAL REASONING

WHAT IS MISSING?

The top pictures go together in some way. Which picture would make the bottom pictures go together in the same way that the top pictures do?

7.

 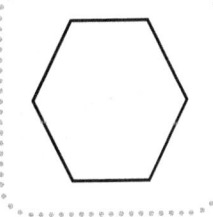    

8.

 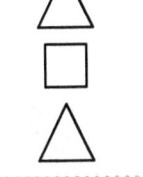 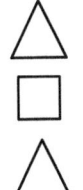  

WHAT IS MISSING?

The top pictures go together in some way. Which picture would make the bottom pictures go together in the same way that the top pictures do?

9.

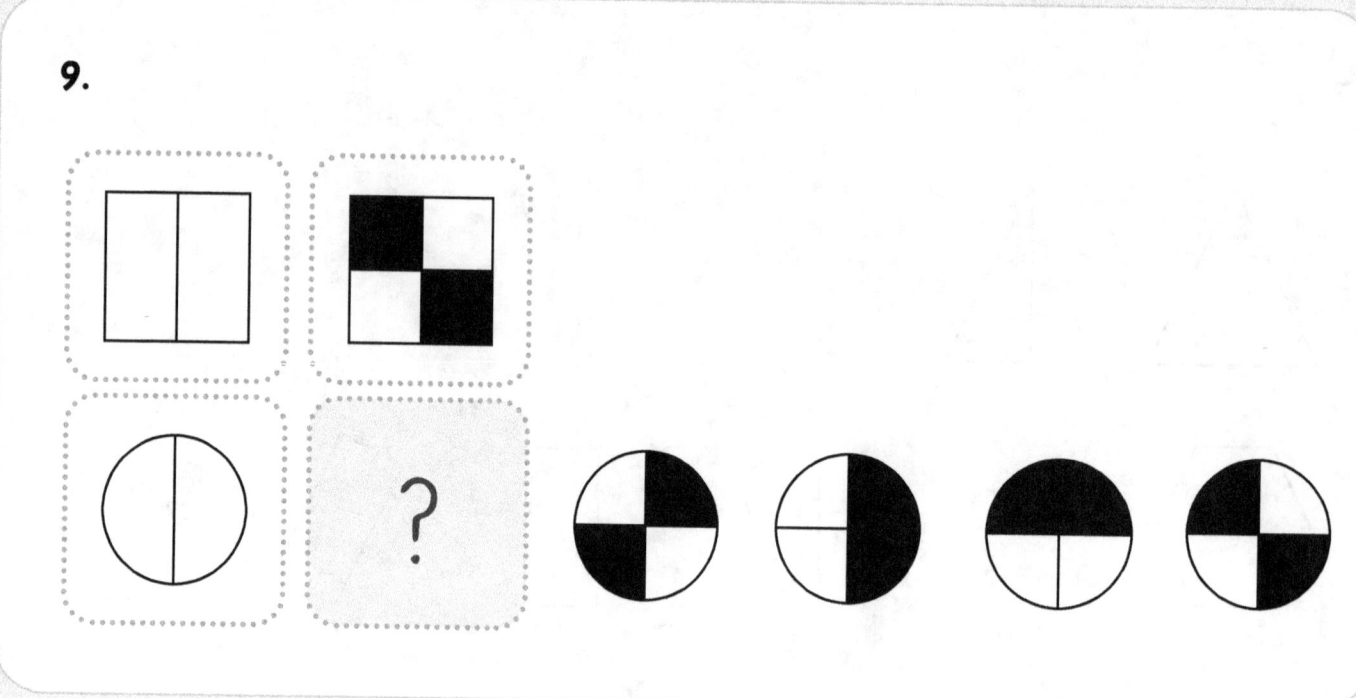

10.

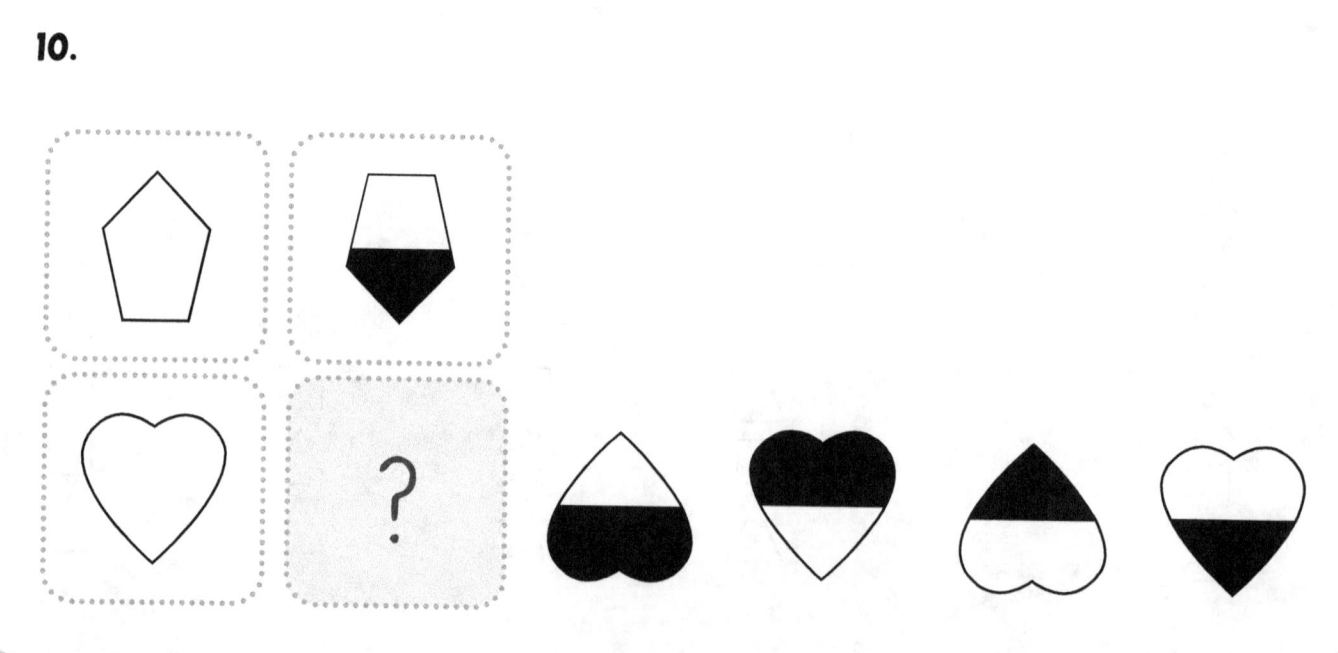

SPATIAL REASONING

WHAT IS MISSING?

The top pictures go together in some way. Which picture would make the bottom pictures go together in the same way that the top pictures do?

11.

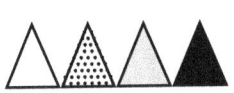

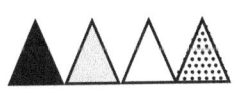

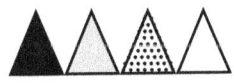

12.

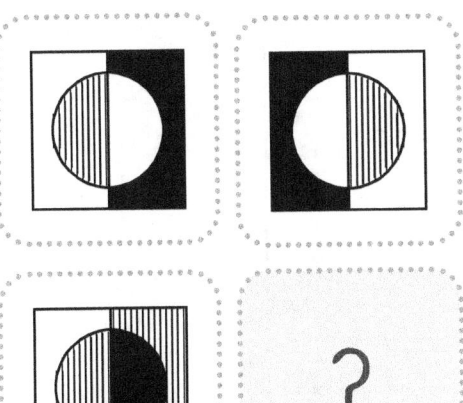

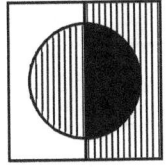

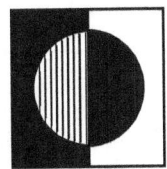

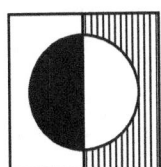

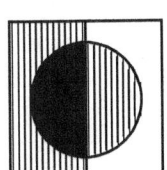

PUZZLE PIECES

Can you find the missing puzzle piece? (Parent note: In the Answer Key, Choice 1 = A, Choice 2 = B, Choice 3 = C, Choice 4 = D, Choice 5 = E.)

1. EXAMPLE

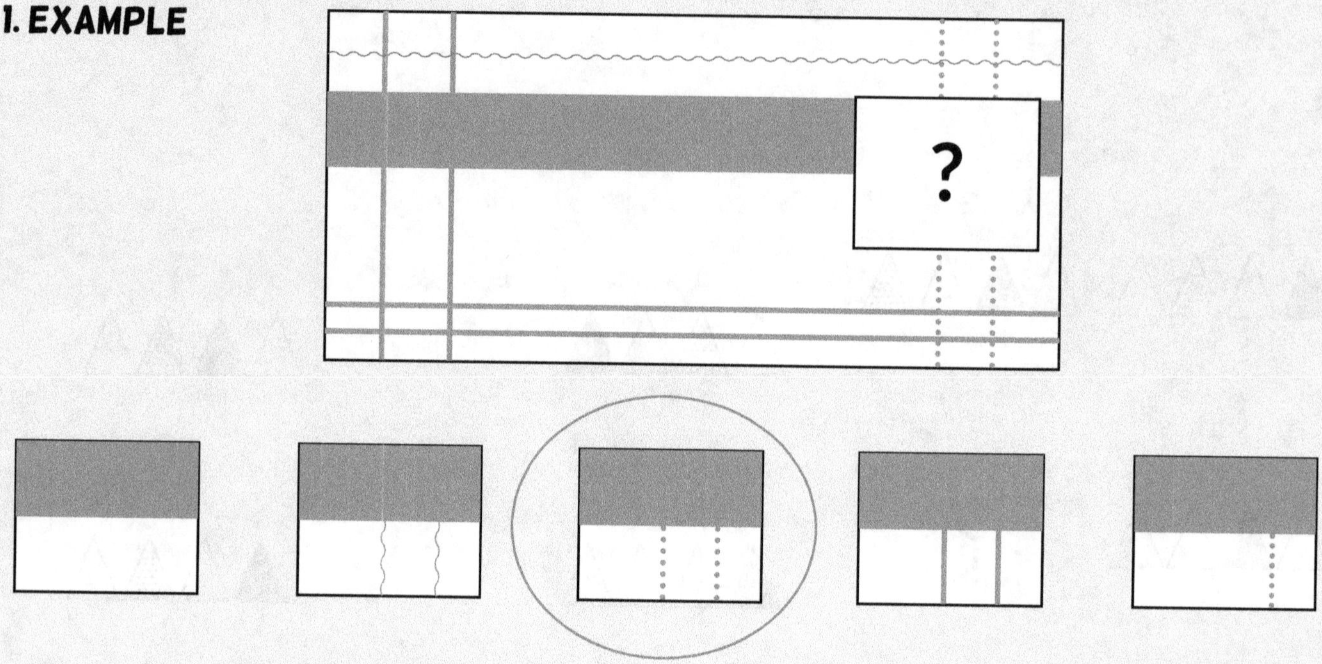

2.

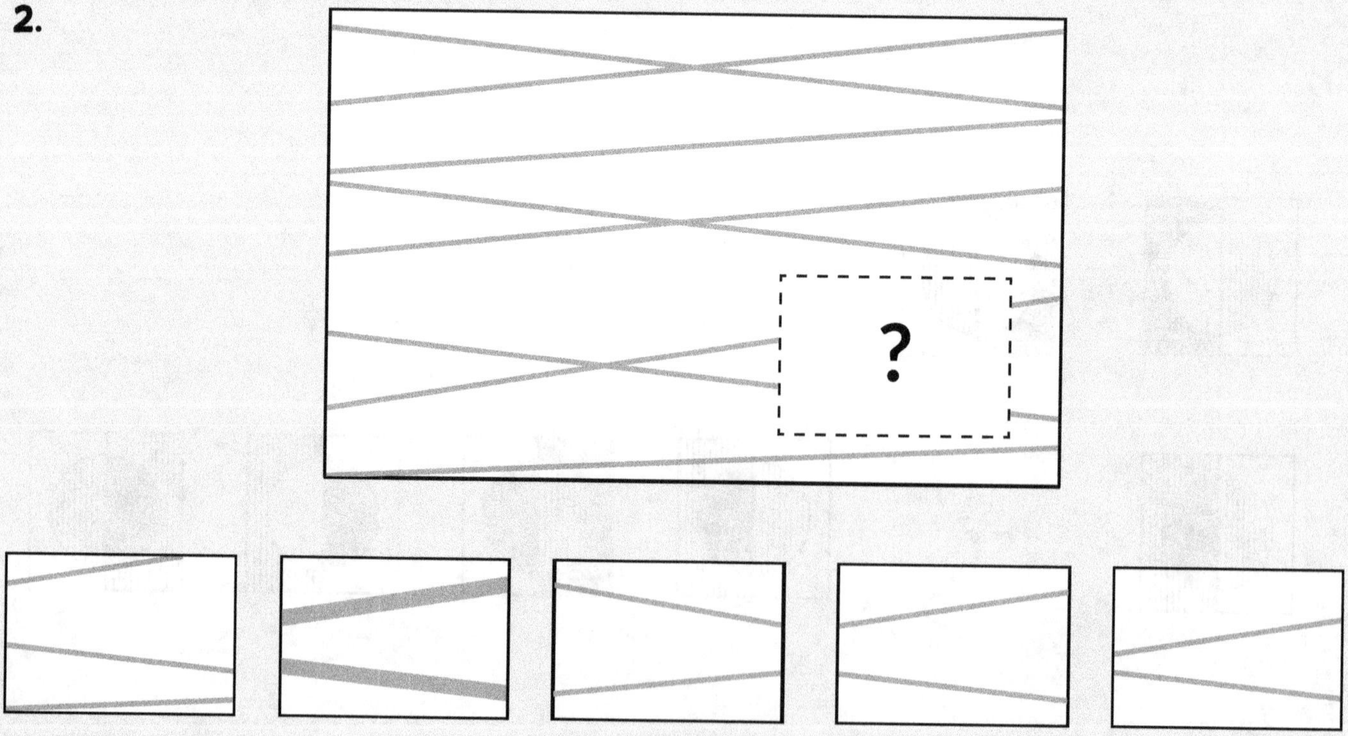

SPATIAL REASONING

PUZZLE PIECES

Can you find the missing puzzle piece?

3.

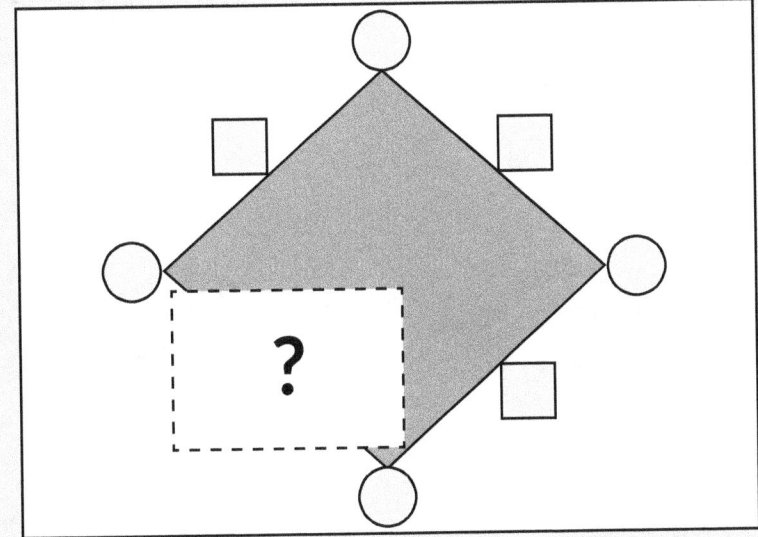

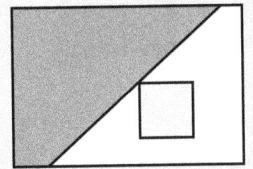 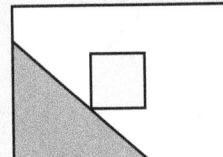 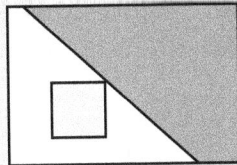 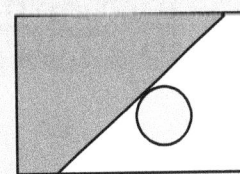 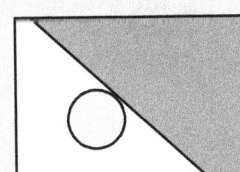

4.

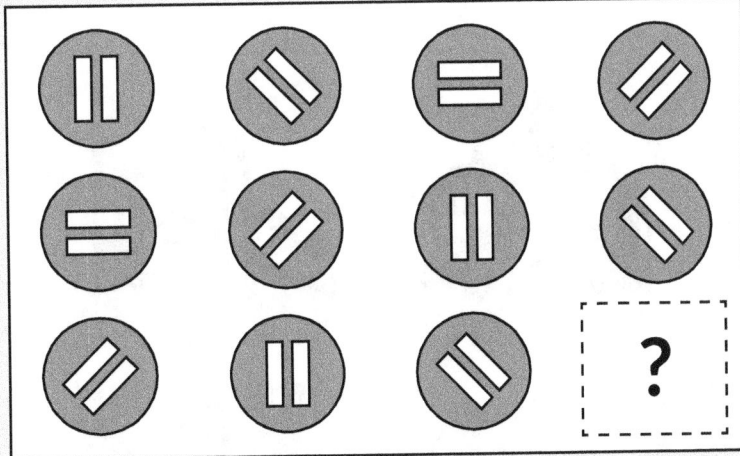

    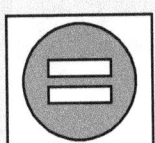

SPATIAL REASONING

23

CAN YOU MATCH?

Can you match the top of the building to the bottom of the building?

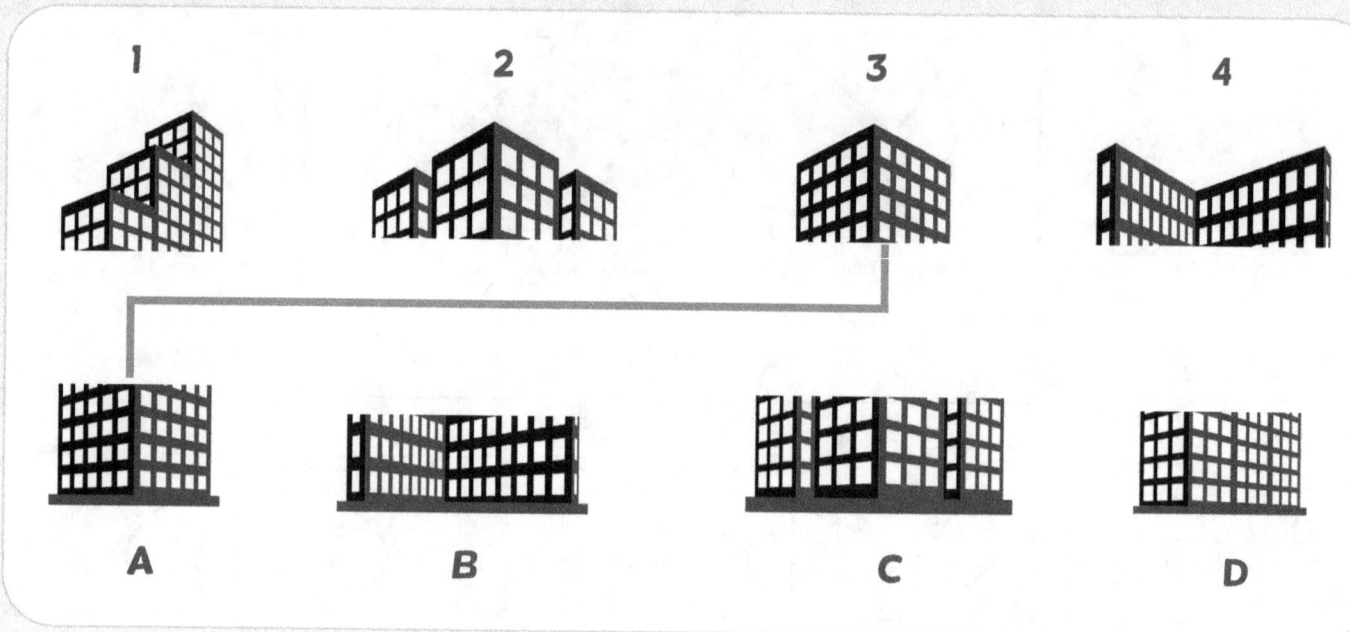

SPATIAL REASONING

CAN YOU MATCH?

Can you match the left half of the magnifying glass to the right half of the magnifying glass?

1

2

3

4

5

A

B

C

D

E

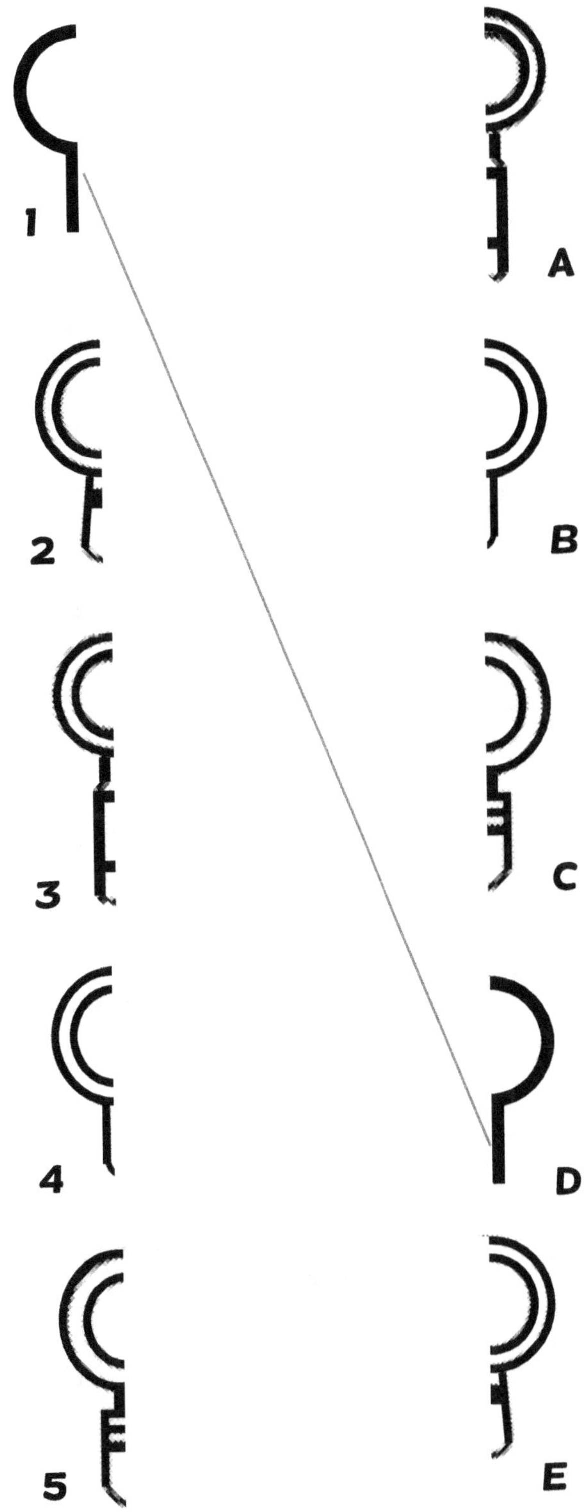

CAN YOU MATCH?

Can you match the top half of the shape to the bottom part?

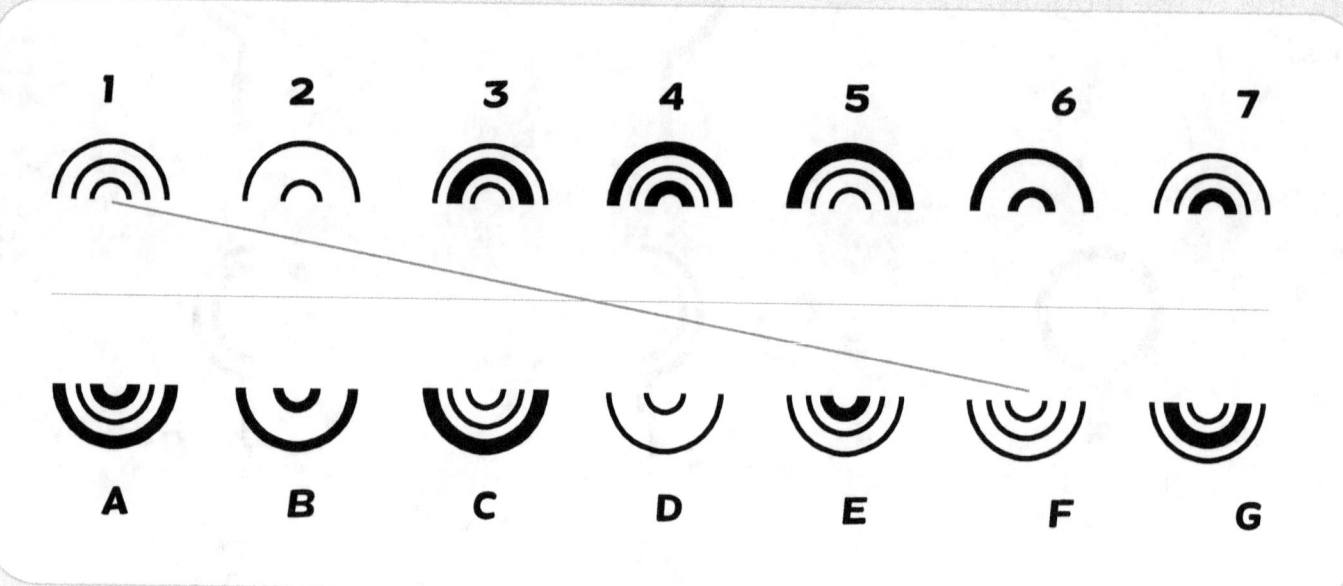

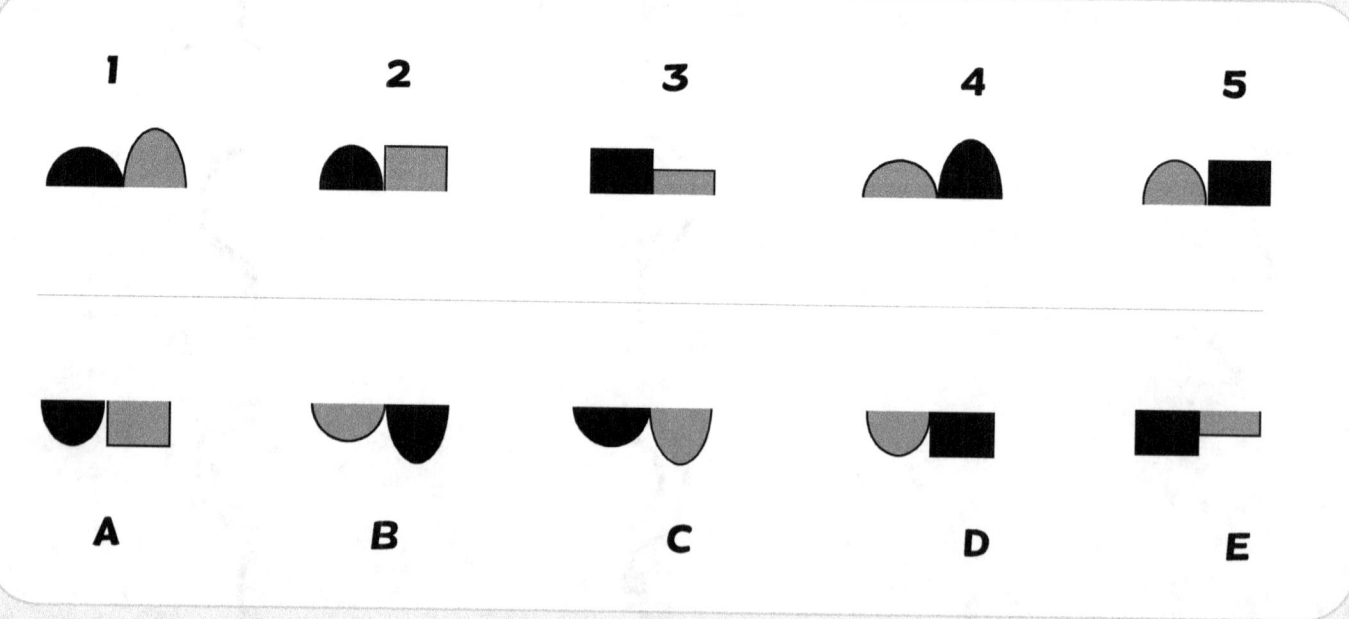

SPATIAL REASONING

ARE YOU A COPYCAT?

Can you copy the pictures?

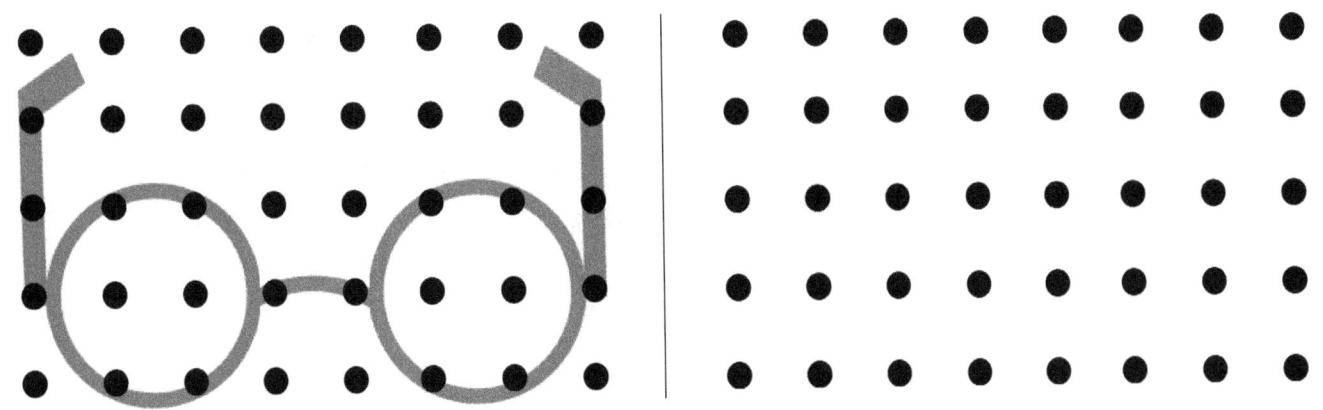

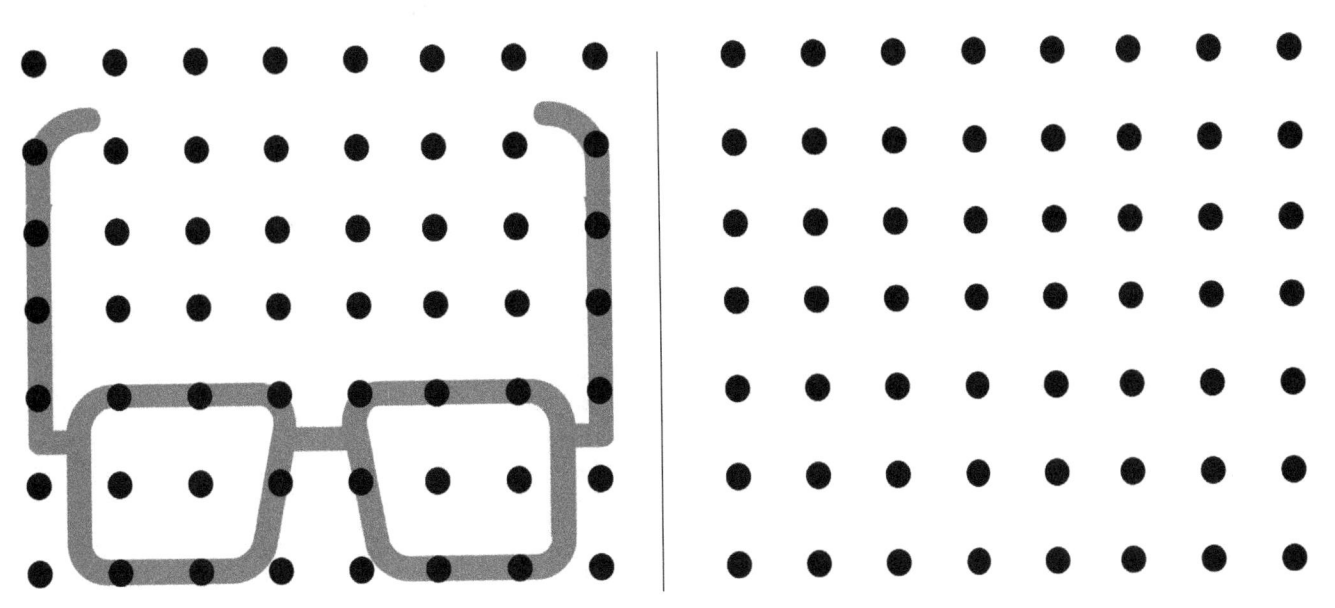

ABOUT IDENTIFICATION
for parents and educators

The activities in the Identification section are meant to build your child's concentration and abilities in noticing details.

Dr. Maria Montessori explained, "The first essential for the child's development is concentration."

By building concentration skills, your child will be better able to analyze information, identify patterns, and make connections between different pieces of information.

Identification skills are developed in this section through:

- Matching objects in images
- Finding differences in images
- Finding shapes in images
- Replication

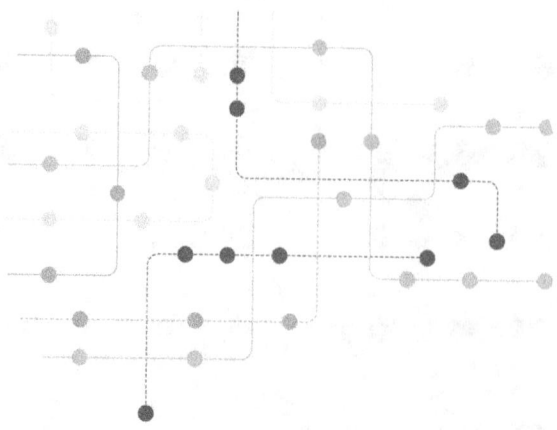

SECTION 2

IDENTIFICATION

You'll never earn enough points!

Sly, the villain, still doesn't think you'll earn enough points to join the Super Sleuths...but we know he's wrong!

Don't forget: after doing each page, check the box at the bottom:

29 ☑

You earn 1 point for each page you do.

CAN YOU FIND THE HIDDEN OBJECTS?

Circle these objects in the city pictures on pages 30 and 31.

Example:

Ferris
Wheel

Lighthouse

Pagoda

Statue
1

Statue
2

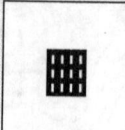
Building
Windows

Tower
Section

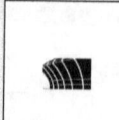
Arena
Section

TOKYO

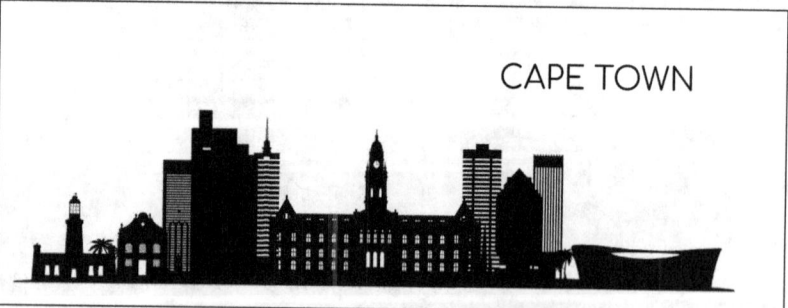
CAPE TOWN

RIO

IDENTIFICATION

CAN YOU FIND THE HIDDEN OBJECTS?

BUENOS AIRES

PARIS

LONDON

DUBAI

CAN YOU SPOT THE DIFFERENCE?

There are 10 things in the top picture that are not in the bottom picture.
Can you find them in the top picture and circle them?

IDENTIFICATION

CAN YOU FIND THE MISSING PIECE?

Can you match the footprint and its missing piece? Write the missing piece's letter.

1

2

3

4

5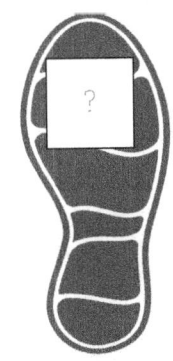

6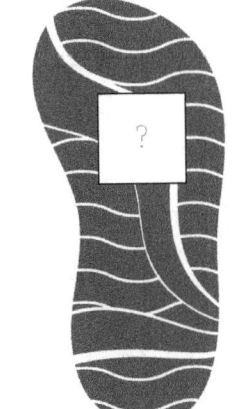

7

A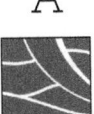

B

C

D

E

F

G

H

I

J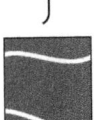

K

L

IDENTIFICATION

33

CAN YOU SPOT THE DIFFERENCE?

There are 10 things in the top picture are not in the bottom picture. Can you find them and circle them?

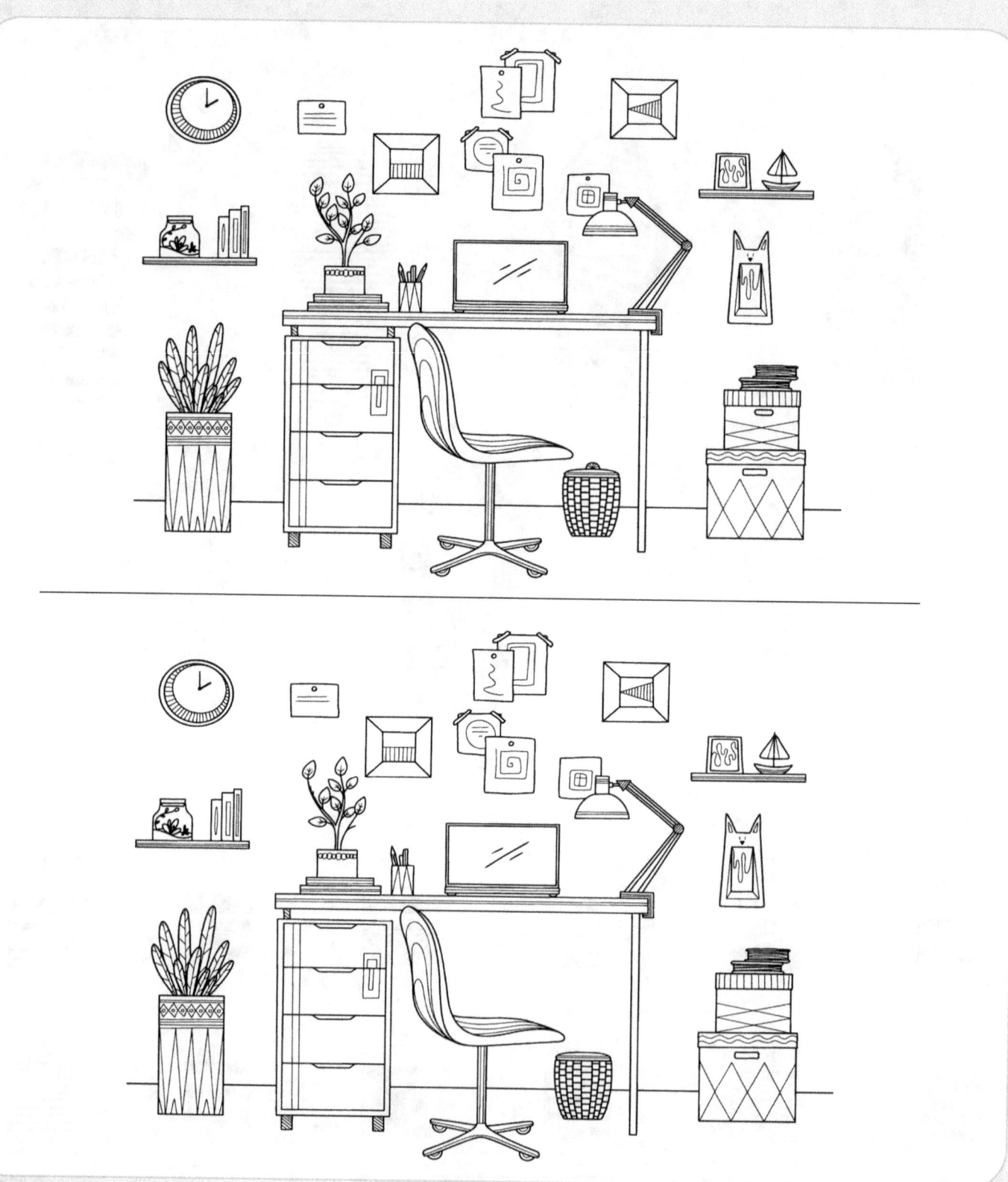

34

CAN YOU FIND THE SHAPES?

Can you find the below shapes in the detective office? (They will be the same size in the office picture at the bottom of the page.)

Shapes

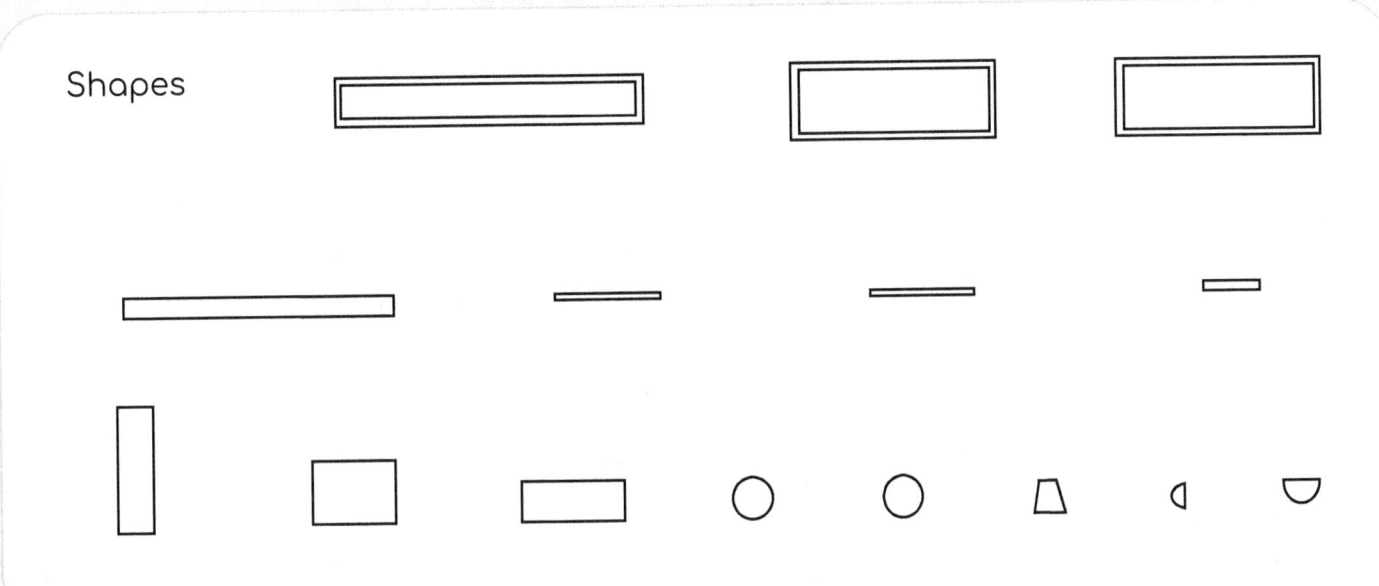

Detective Office

ABOUT PATTERNS & SEQUENCING
for parents and educators

In these activities, your child will determine what comes next in a pattern or in a sequence.

Your child will identify relationships and make sense of information. This information may at first appear rather simple but is actually quite complex.

Recognizing patterns will improve your child's ability in drawing conclusions and making predictions- essential skills for problem-solving and critical thinking.

Pattern and sequencing skills are developed in this section in activities like:

- "What Comes Next?" (in a pattern)
- "What Comes Next?" (in a sequence of events)
- Sudoku

You may have made it this far, but you'll never finish the rest!

Sly doesn't think you can finish the rest, but we know he's wrong!

Don't forget: after doing each page, check the box at the bottom:

 38

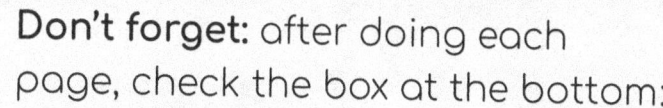 You earn 1 point for each page you do.

37

WHAT COMES NEXT?

The row of pictures has made a pattern. A picture is missing. Can you draw what picture would finish the pattern?

1. EXAMPLE

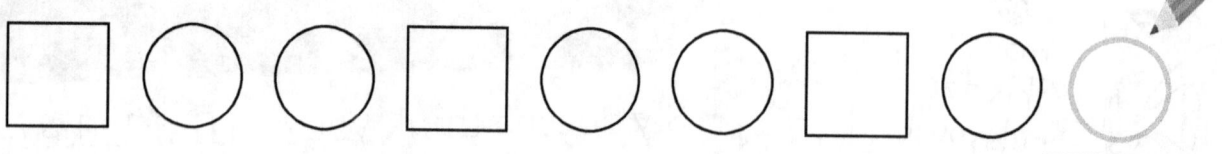

2.

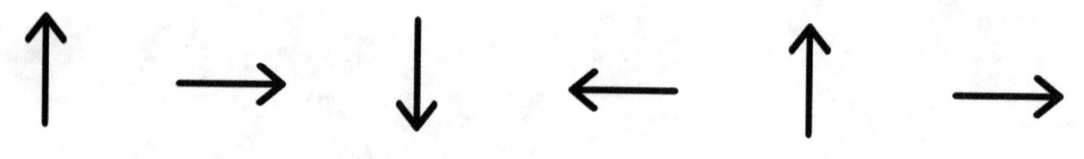

3.

PATTERNS & SEQUENCING

WHAT COMES NEXT?

The row of pictures has made a pattern. A picture is missing. Can you draw what picture would finish the pattern?

4.

5.

6.

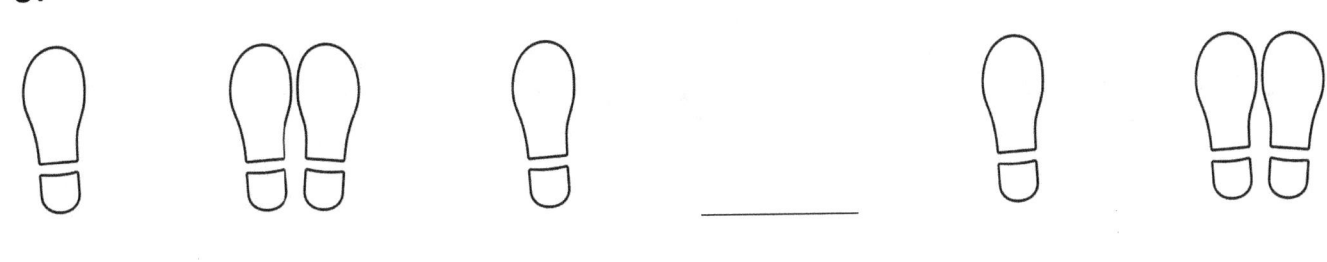

WHAT COMES NEXT?

The row of pictures has made a pattern. A picture is missing. Can you draw what picture would finish the pattern?

7.

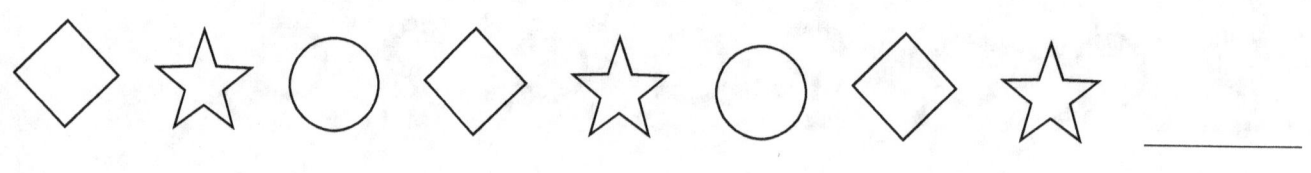

8.

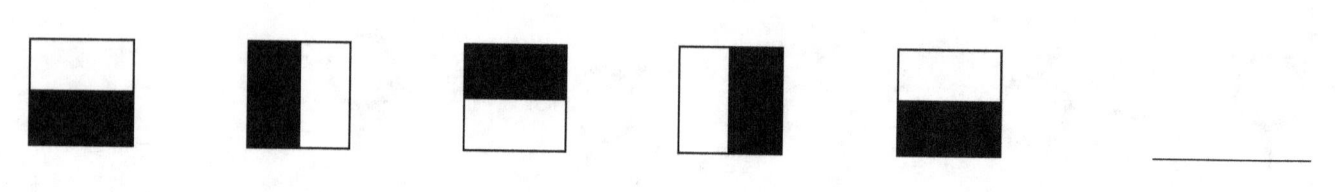

9.

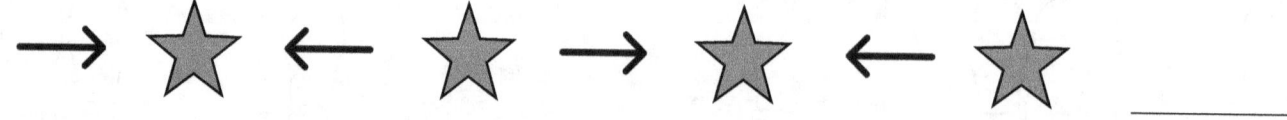

PATTERNS & SEQUENCING

WHAT COMES NEXT?

The row of pictures has made a pattern. A picture is missing. Can you draw what picture would finish the pattern?

10.

↑↑↑↑   ↑↑↑↓   ↑↑↓↓   ↑↓↓↓   _____

11.

↑   ↓↓   ↑↑↑   ↓↓↓↓   _____

12.

A   B   C
B   C   A
C   A   B   _____

WHAT COMES NEXT?

The row of pictures has made a pattern. A picture is missing. Can you figure out what picture would finish the pattern? Circle your choice.
(In the Answer Key, Choice 1 = A, Choice 2 = B, Choice 3 = C.)

13. EXAMPLE

    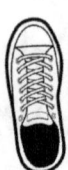    _____

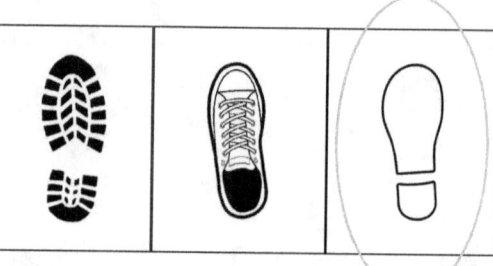

14.

     _____

PATTERNS & SEQUENCING

WHAT COMES NEXT?

The row of pictures has made a pattern. A picture is missing. Can you figure out what picture would finish the pattern? (Circle your choice.)

15.

   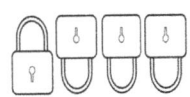 _____

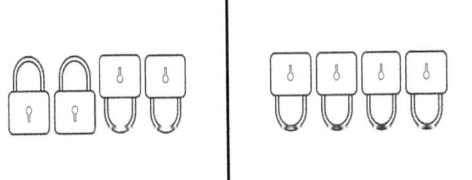

16.

 _____

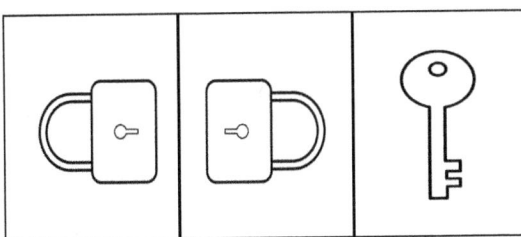

WHAT COMES NEXT?

The row of pictures has made a pattern. A picture is missing. Can you figure out what picture would finish the pattern? (Circle your choice.)

17.

 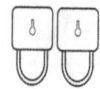  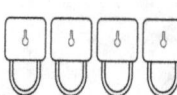 _____

 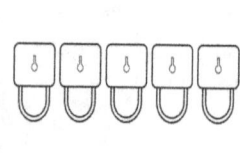 

18.

   _____

PATTERNS & SEQUENCING

WHAT COMES NEXT?

Which picture would come next? (Circle your choice.)

19.

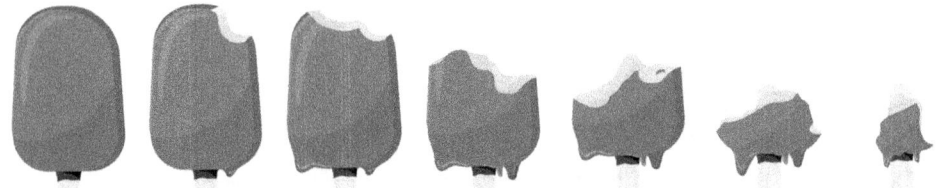

20.

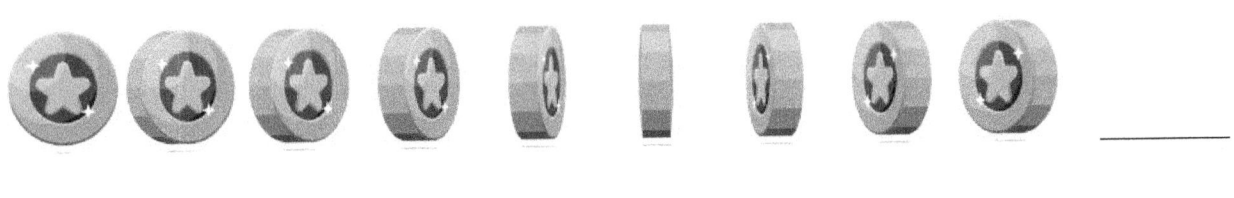

SUDOKU

Finish the grid so that each row and each column has each picture only one time. You cannot move the pictures that are already below.

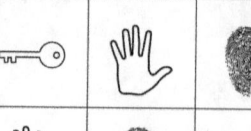
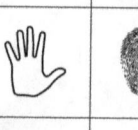
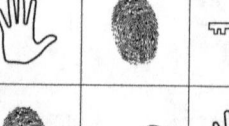

 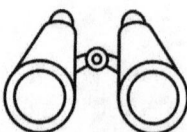 

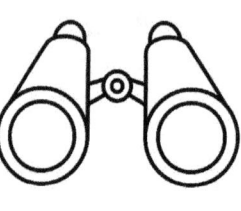

PATTERNS & SEQUENCING

SUDOKU

Finish the grid so that each row and each column has each picture only one time. You cannot move the pictures that are already below.

 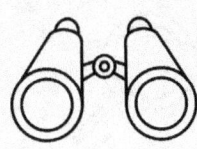  

SUDOKU

Finish the grid so that each row and each column has each picture only one time. You cannot move the pictures that are already below.

 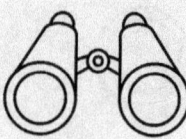  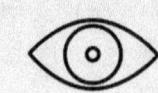

PATTERNS & SEQUENCING

SUDOKU

Finish the grid so that each row and each column has each picture only one time. You cannot move the pictures that are already below.

 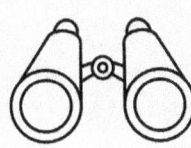  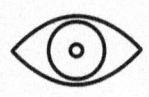

ABOUT VERBAL REASONING
for parents and educators

In these activities, your child will determine the relationship between a group of pictures. Then, they will make a decision based on this relationship (either which picture does not belong or which picture would come next).

Because children have different reading abilities, questions are picture-based, instead of word-based.

Verbal reasoning skills are developed in this section with these activities:

- Verbal Classification ("Which One Does Not Belong?")

- Verbal Analogies ("What Is Missing?")

SECTION 4

VERBAL REASONING

Don't forget: after doing each page, check the box at the bottom:

You earn 1 point for each page you do.

WHICH ONE DOES NOT BELONG?

These pictures are alike in some way, except for one picture. Can you figure out which picture does not belong?

Example: Let's figure out what each of the pictures (except for one) have in common. They are worn on the head, except the sweater. So, let's cross out the sweater.

(Parent note: The answer choices are not labelled A, B, C, etc. In the Answer Key, Choice 1 = A, Choice 2 = B, Choice 3 = C, Choice 4 = D, Choice 5 = E.)

1. EXAMPLE

2.

WHICH ONE DOES NOT BELONG?

These pictures are alike in some way, except for one picture. Can you figure out which picture does not belong?

3.

4.

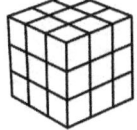    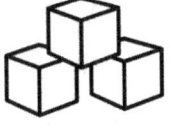

WHICH ONE DOES NOT BELONG?

These pictures are alike in some way, except for one picture. Can you figure out which picture does not belong?

5.

6.

VERBAL REASONING

WHICH ONE DOES NOT BELONG?

These pictures are alike in some way, except for one picture. Can you figure out which picture does not belong?

7.

 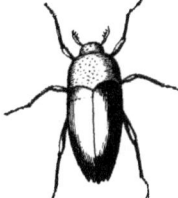   

8.

WHICH ONE DOES NOT BELONG?

These pictures are alike in some way, except for one picture. Can you figure out which picture does not belong?

9.

10.

VERBAL REASONING

WHICH ONE DOES NOT BELONG?

These pictures are alike in some way, except for one picture. Can you figure out which picture does not belong?

11.

12.

 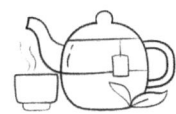  

WHAT IS MISSING?

The top pictures go together in some way. Which picture would make the bottom pictures go together in the same way that the top pictures do? Circle your answer.

Example (#1): Look at the 2 pictures on top. "Magnifying glass" is to "eye" as "headphones" are to ...? Let's try to come up with a "rule" that describes how these go together. The thing in the first box is used with the part of your body in the second box. How would we use this rule with the thing in the bottom box (the headphones)? Headphones are used with your ear.

1. EXAMPLE

2.

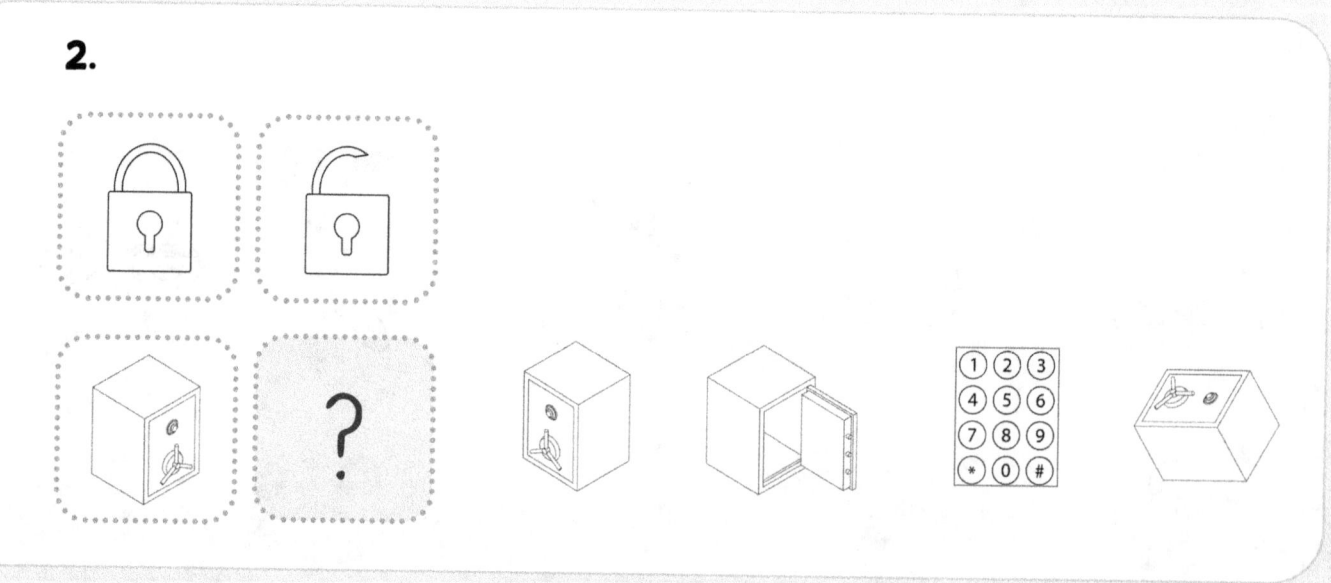

VERBAL REASONING

WHAT IS MISSING?

The top pictures go together in some way. Which picture would make the bottom pictures go together in the same way that the top pictures do? Circle your answer.

3.

4.

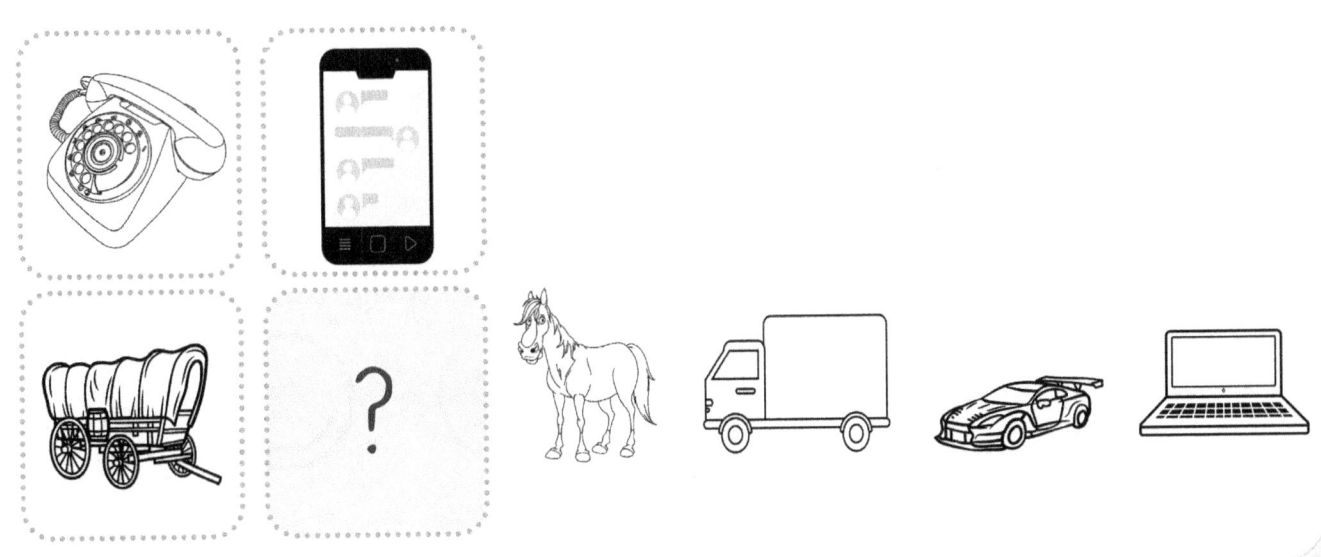

WHAT IS MISSING?

The top pictures go together in some way. Which picture would make the bottom pictures go together in the same way that the top pictures do? Circle your answer.

5.

6.

VERBAL REASONING

WHAT IS MISSING?

The top pictures go together in some way. Which picture would make the bottom pictures go together in the same way that the top pictures do? Circle your answer.

7.

8.

ABOUT QUANTITATIVE REASONING
for parents and educators

Quantitative reasoning exercises go beyond the math activities your child usually does in school.

These require not only counting and computing, but also finding relationships, comparing, and determining what comes next in a series.

Quantitative reasoning skills are developed in this section with these activities:

- Can You Balance? (Using addition, subtraction, basic multiplication/division)
- How Many Keys? (Determining mathematical patterns)
- How Many Sweets? (Equation building)
- What Is Missing? (Mathematical analogies)

SECTION 5
QUANTITATIVE REASONING

SHOW SLY THAT
YOU WON'T GIVE UP!

Don't forget: after doing each
page, check the box at the bottom:

You earn 1 point for each page you do.

CAN YOU BALANCE?

Can you figure out the missing numbers? (The scales must balance, meaning both sides must be equal.)

EXAMPLE

1.

8

14

?

 = _4_

 = _10_

? = _10_

2.

6

12

?

 = _____

 = _____

? = _____

QUANTITATIVE REASONING

CAN YOU BALANCE?

Can you figure out the missing numbers? (The scales must balance, meaning both sides must be equal.)

3.

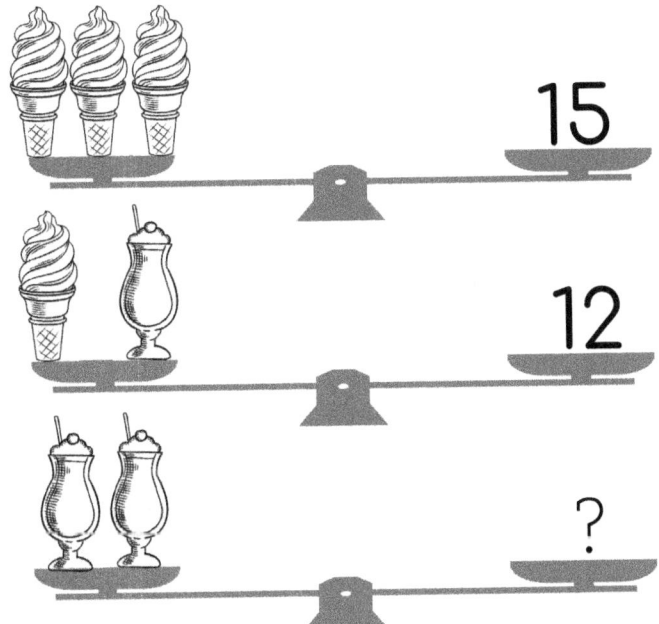

15

12

?

 = _____

 = _____

? = _____

4.

24

13

?

= _____

= _____

? = _____

CAN YOU BALANCE?

Can you figure out the missing numbers? (The scales must balance, meaning both sides must be equal.)

5.

 30

 14

 ?

🧁 = _____

🍰 = _____

? = _____

6.

 10

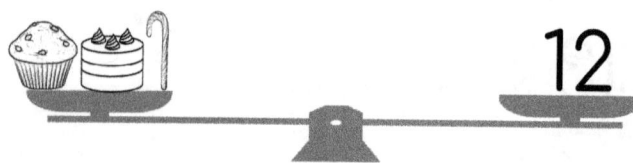 12

 ?

🧁🍰 = _____

🍬 = _____

? = _____

QUANTITATIVE REASONING

CAN YOU BALANCE?

Can you figure out the missing numbers? (The scales must balance, meaning both sides must be equal.)

7.

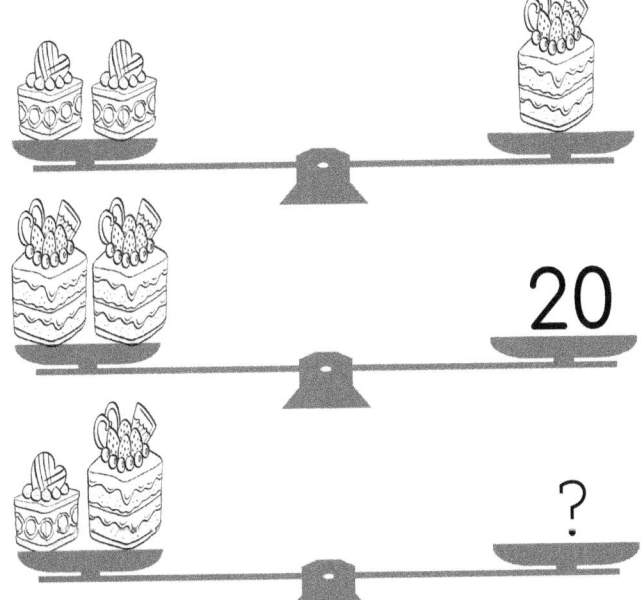

20

?

 = _____

 = _____

? = _____

8.

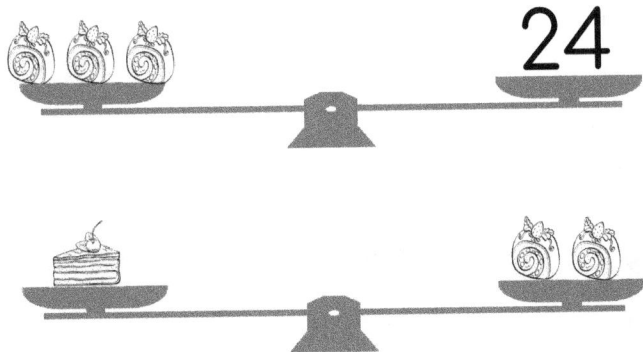

24

?

 = _____

 = _____

? = _____

HOW MANY KEYS?

Look at the number of keys in each column. (The number is at the bottom of each column.) They have made a pattern. Can you figure out how many keys come next in the pattern?

Example (#1): Look at each column and the number below it. They have made a pattern. In each column, one is added. How many keys would come next in the pattern? It would be 6.

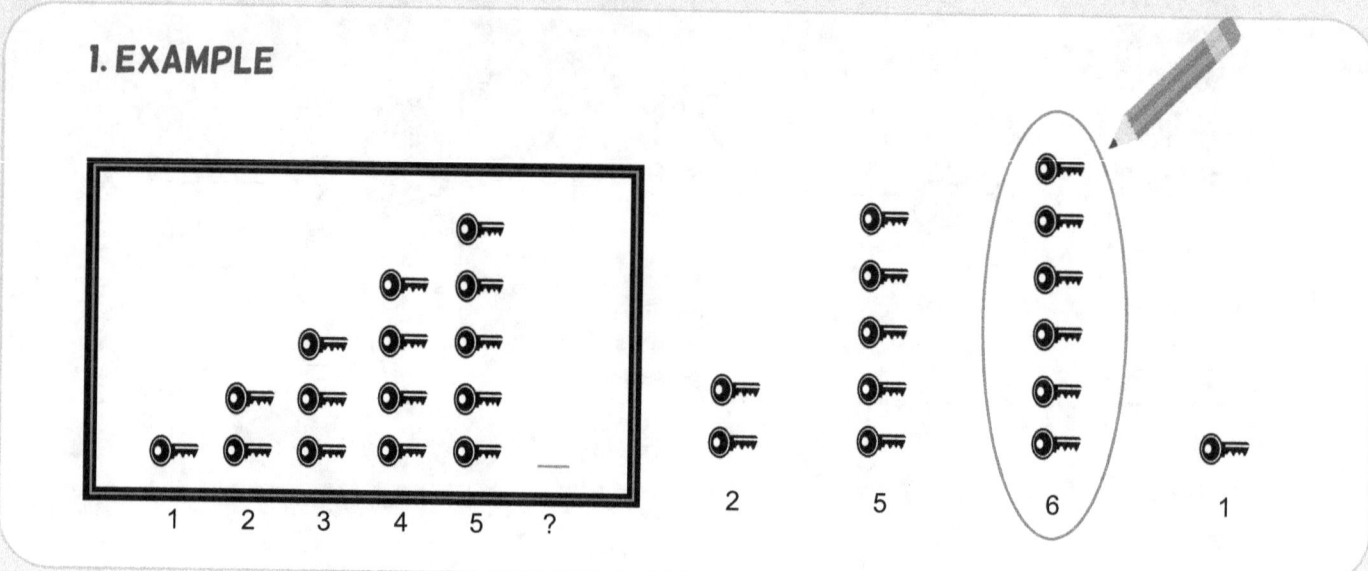

1. EXAMPLE

1   2   3   4   5   ?

2   5   6   1

2.

2   5   2   5   2   ?

2   5   4   1

QUANTITATIVE REASONING

HOW MANY KEYS?

Look at the number of keys in each column. (The number is at the bottom of each column.) They have made a pattern. Can you figure out how many keys come next in the pattern?

3.

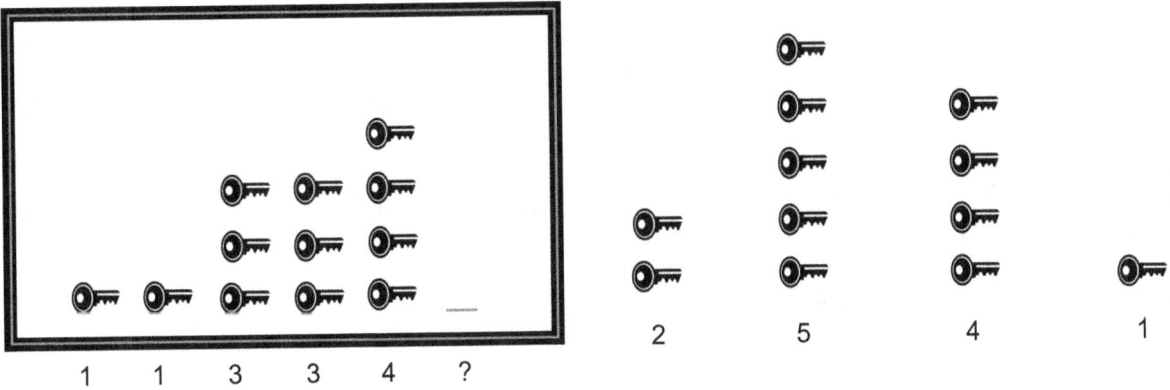

4.

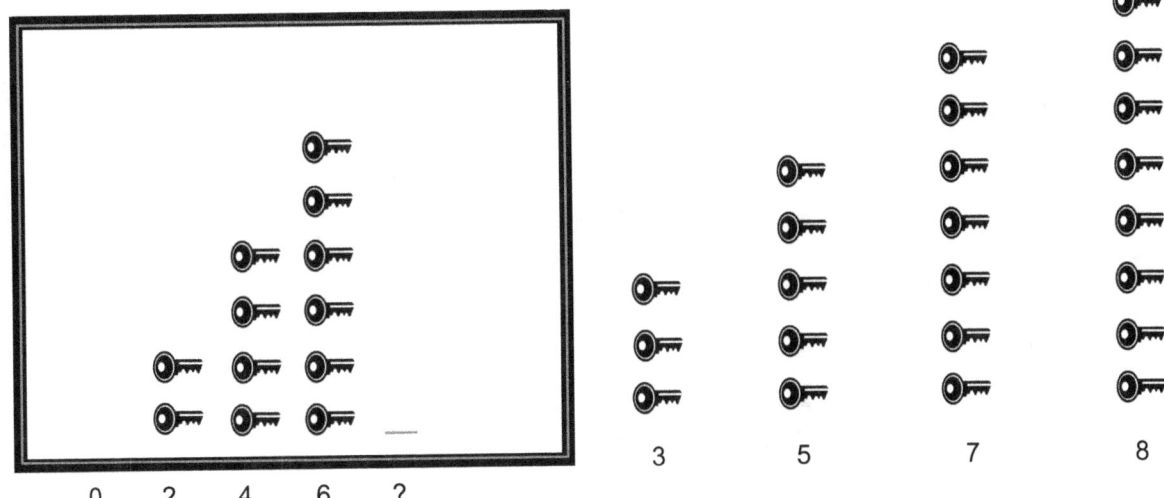

HOW MANY KEYS?

Look at the number of keys in each column. (The number is at the bottom of each column.) They have made a pattern. Can you figure out how many keys come next in the pattern?

5.

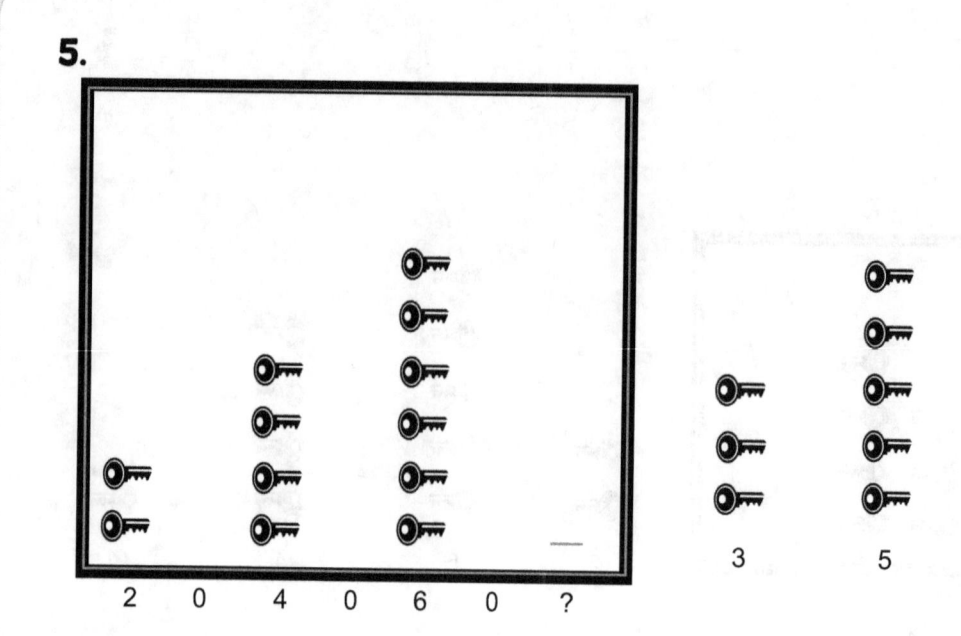

2 0 4 0 6 0 ?

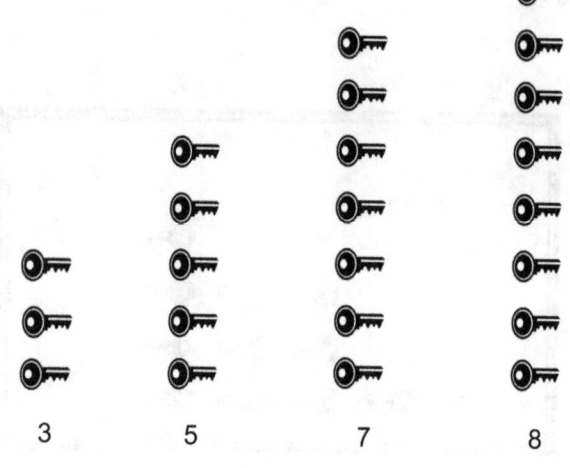

3 5 7 8

6.

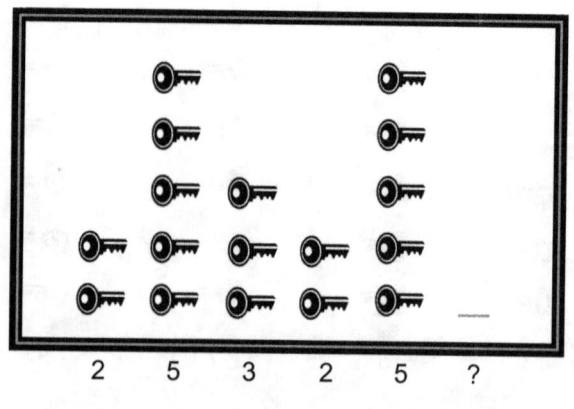

2 5 3 2 5 ?

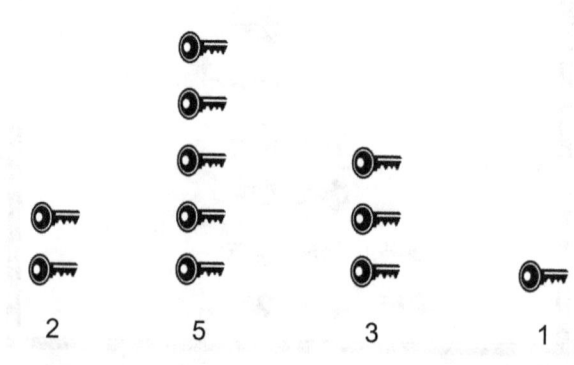

2 5 3 1

QUANTITATIVE REASONING

HOW MANY KEYS?

Look at the number of keys in each column. (The number is at the bottom of each column.) They have made a pattern. Can you figure out how many keys come next in the pattern?

7.

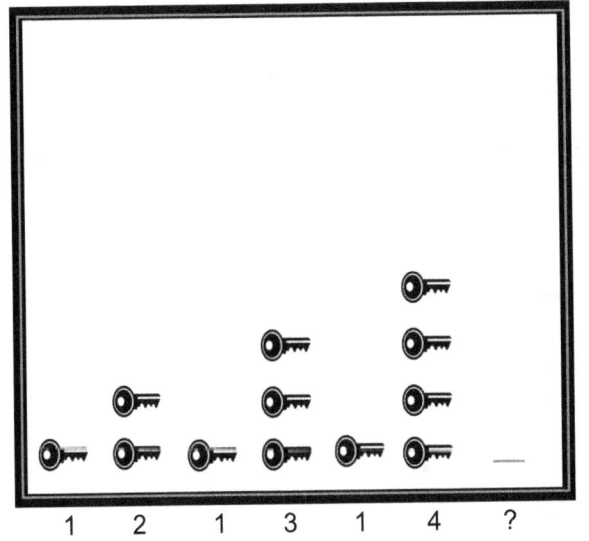

1	2	1	3	1	4	?

3   5   7   1

8.

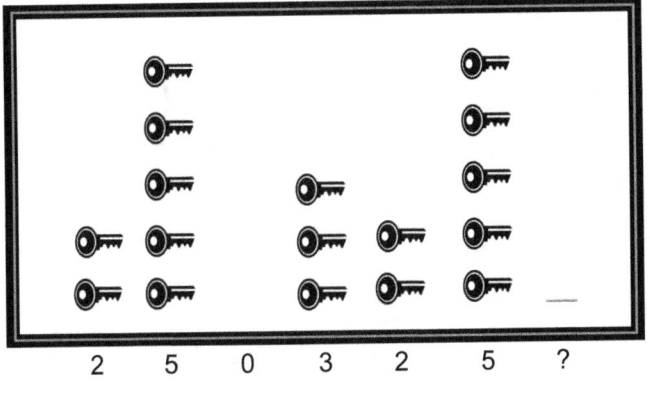

2	5	0	3	2	5	?

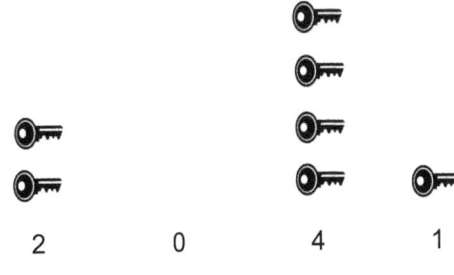

2   0   4   1

HOW MANY SWEETS?

Can you figure out how much each sweet is worth?

1. EXAMPLE

🍭 + 🍭 = __20__   🍭 = __10__

🍭 + 🍭 = __16__   🍭 = __8__

🍭 + 🍬 = __22__   🍬 = __12__

🍭 + ⚪ = __19__   ⚪ = __9__

🍭 + 🍭 − ⚪ = __9__

🍭 + 🍭 − 🍬 = __6__

QUANTITATIVE REASONING

HOW MANY SWEETS?

Can you figure out how much each sweet is worth?

2.

🍬 + 🍬 + 🍬 = __12__   🍬 = _____

🍩 + 🍩 − 🍬 = __10__   🍩 = _____

🍬 + 🎂 + 🍩 = __30__   🎂 = _____

🎂 − 🍬 − 🍩 = _____

QUANTITATIVE REASONING

73

Critical Thinking

HOW MUCH?

Can you figure out how much the pizza (and drink) are worth?

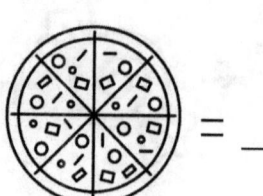

(pizza) + (pizza) = 24

(pizza) = _____

(drink) = _____

(half pizza) + (half pizza) = _____

(quarter pizza) + (quarter pizza) = _____

 + (drink) = 4

 + (drink) = _____

QUANTITATIVE REASONING

WHAT WOULD YOU BUY?

If you had $300, what detective equipment would you buy?
Circle them.

If you bought one of each item, how much would you spend?

$80

$20

$10

$10

$200

$50

WHAT IS MISSING?

The top pictures go together in some way. What changed from the left picture & right picture? (Look at the number of things in the left & right box.) What should go in the bottom right box?

1. HINT: ADD 2.

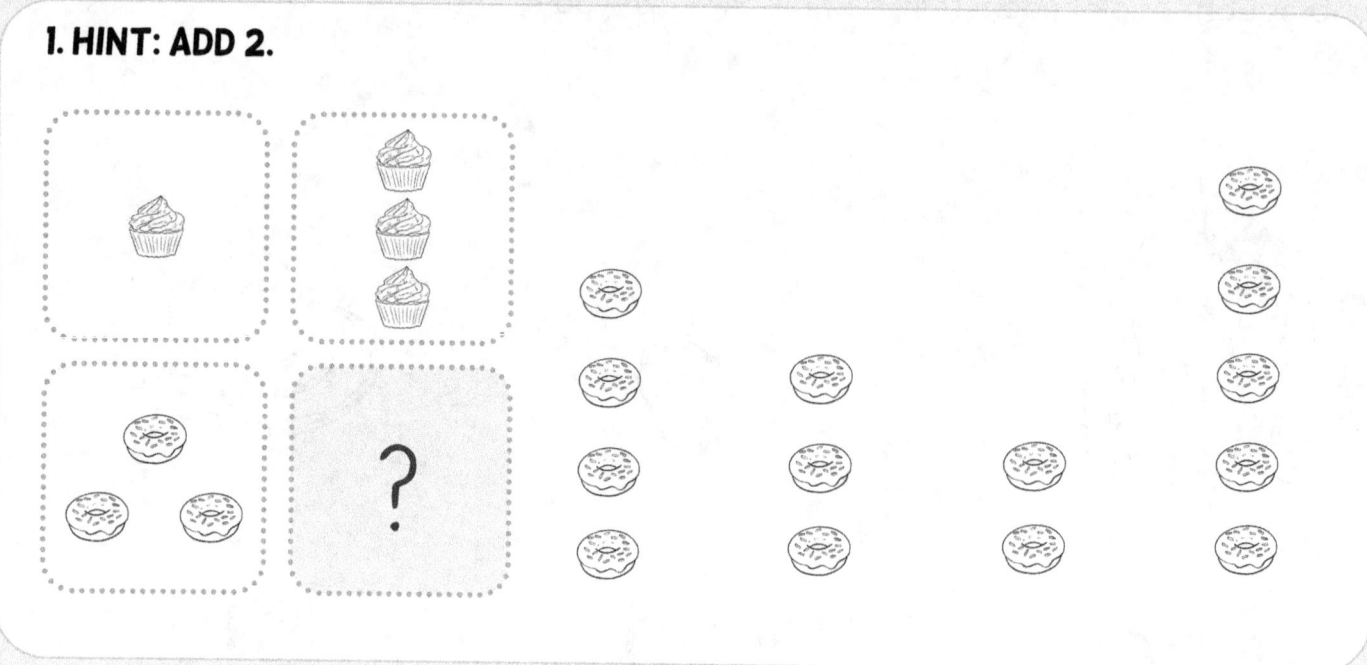

2.

QUANTITATIVE REASONING

WHAT IS MISSING?

The top pictures go together in some way. What changed from the left picture & right picture? (Look at the number of things in the left & right box.) What should go in the bottom right box?

3.

4. HINT: MULTIPLY BY 2.

WHAT IS MISSING?

The top pictures go together in some way. What changed from the left picture & right picture? (Look at the number of things in the left & right box.) What should go in the bottom right box?

5.

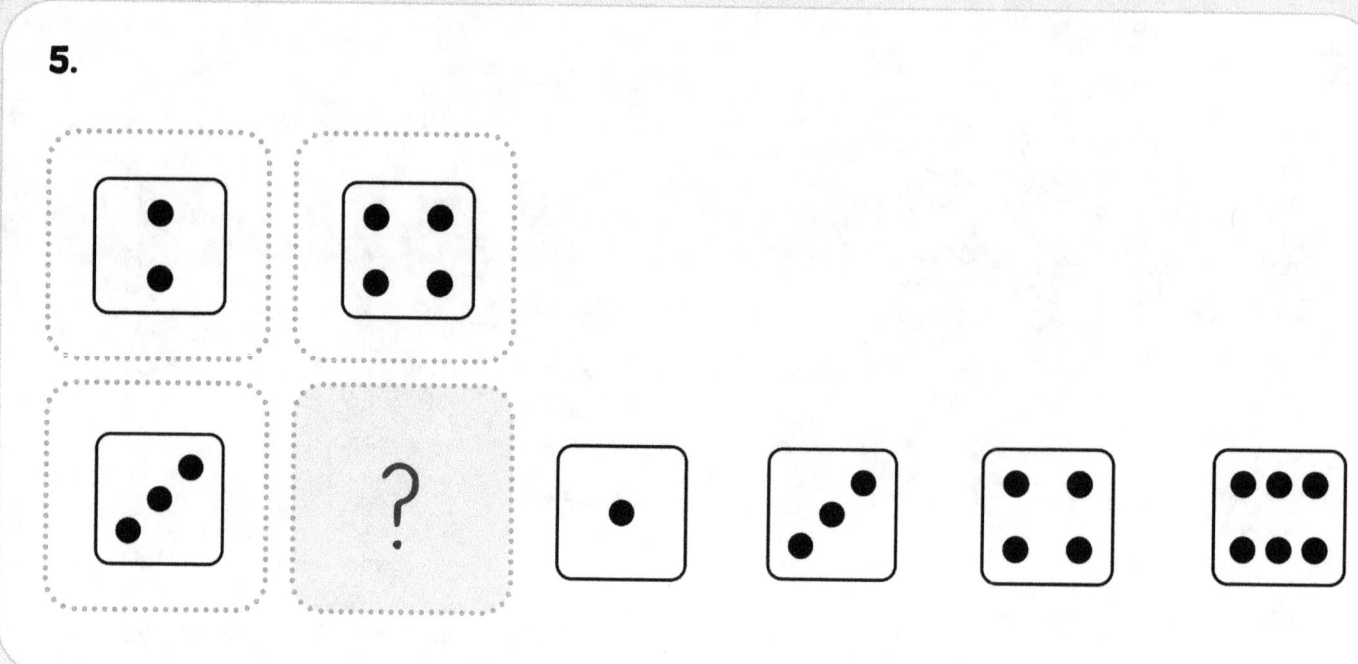

6.

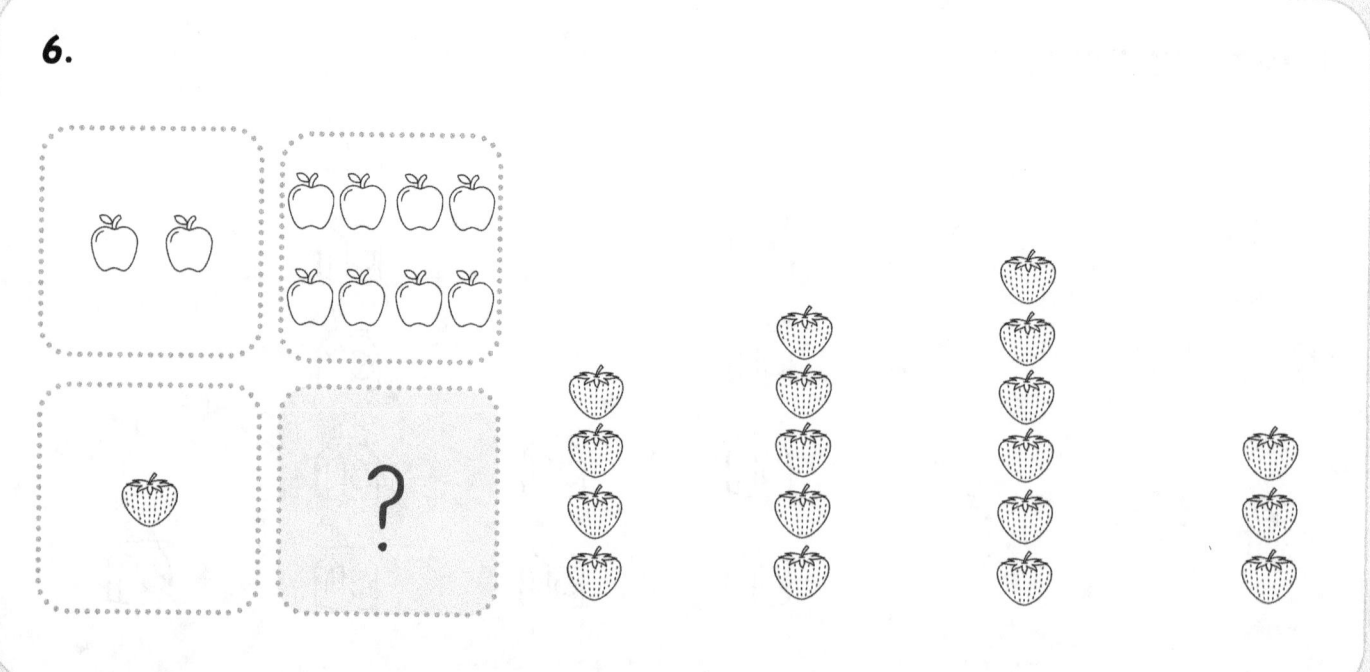

QUANTITATIVE REASONING

WHAT IS MISSING?

The top pictures go together in some way. What changed from the left picture & right picture? (Look at the number of things in the left & right box.) What should go in the bottom right box?

7.

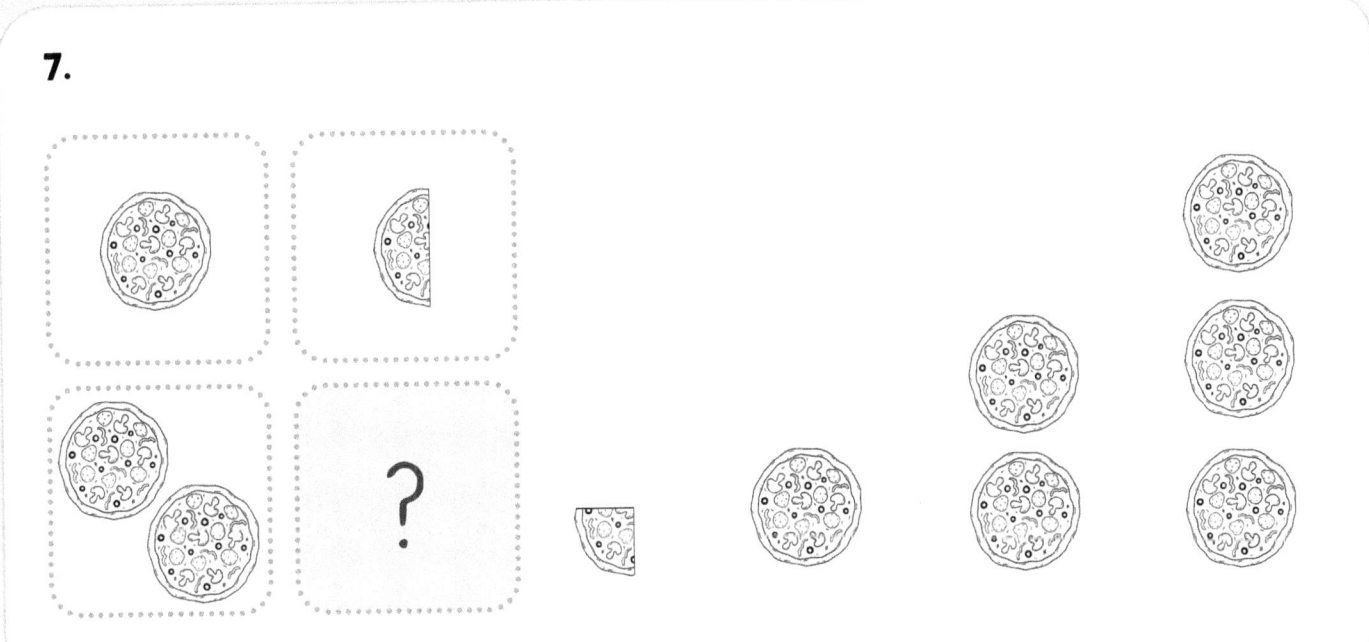

8.

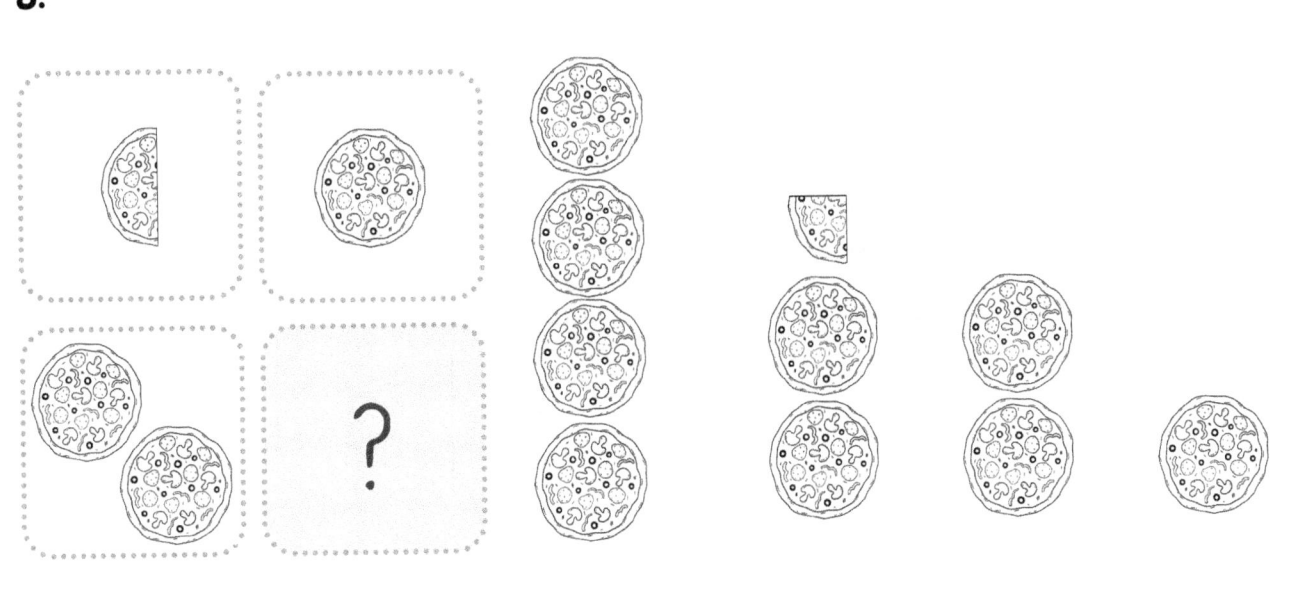

MAGIC SQUARES

All columns, all rows, and all diagonals (with 3 numbers) must add up to the same number. Can you figure out what number goes in the empty spaces?

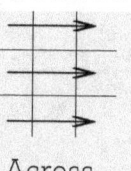 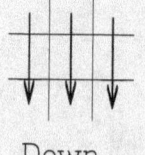 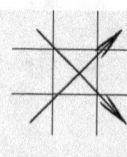

Across   Down   Diagonal

EXAMPLE

2	1	3
3	2	1

All must equal: _____

→

2	1	3
3	2	1
1	*3*	*2*

All must equal: __6__

1.

5		6
6		4
4		5

All must equal: _____

2.

2	7	
	5	
4	3	

All must equal: _____

QUANTITATIVE REASONING

MAGIC SQUARES

All columns, all rows, and all diagonals (with 3 numbers) must add up to the same number. Can you figure out what number goes in the empty spaces?

3.

1	8	
5		
9	4	

All must equal: _____

4.

7	0	8
6		
2	10	

All must equal: _____

5.

4		
8	0	
12	10	

All must equal: _____

6.

10		
	40	20
	0	70

All must equal: _____

WHAT WOULD YOU BUY?

If you had $1,200, what detective equipment would you buy?
Circle them.

If you bought one of each item, how much would you spend?

$500

$200

$10

$400

$500

$200

QUANTITATIVE REASONING

WHAT WOULD YOU BUY?

If you had $1,500, what detective equipment would you buy? Circle them.

$1,000

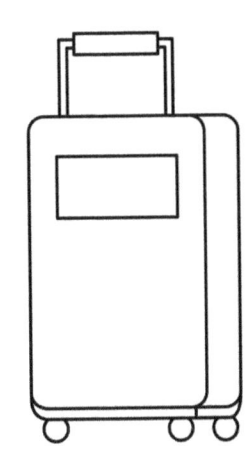

$200

$50

$500

$500

$500

ABOUT LOGIC MATRICES
for parents and educators

A logic matrix refers to a type of puzzle/brain-teaser that challenges your child to use logic to solve complex problems.

These involve a series of clues/information that must be analyzed to arrive at a solution.

These activities improve problem-solving abilities and promote mental agility.

You may read the information to your child. (Or, if your child has a high enough reading level, your child may read.)

Be sure to look at the explanation on p.87 which explains how to use the grids to arrive at the correct answer.

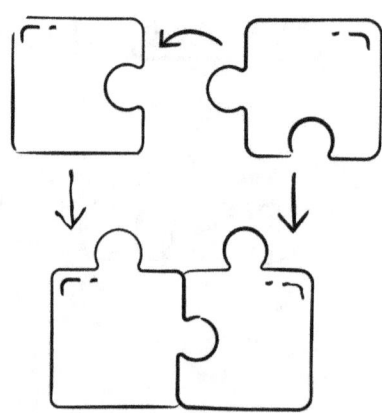

SECTION 5

LOGIC MATRICES

You only have a few more to go.

Aren't you going to give up?

ONLY A FEW MORE. WE KNOW YOU CAN DO IT!

Don't forget: after doing each page, check the box at the bottom:

85 ☑

You earn 1 point for each page you do.

WHAT'S THEIR FAVORITE ANIMAL?

Figure out each detective's favorite animal by reading the clues below. (Each detective has a different favorite animal.)

Clues:

• Lee's favorite animal likes to sit on people's shoulders.

• Ana's favorite animal has legs and so does Lee's favorite animal.

Tips:
1. Carefully read the clues.
2. As you read, draw a check mark to mark the things that are true.
3. As you read, draw an X to mark the things that are not true.

LOGIC MATRICES

EXPLANATION

-Clue 1 says, "Lee's favorite animal likes to sit on people's shoulders."

-So, put a check mark where Lee & the bird cross. We know this is Lee's favorite animal.

-That means we can put an X where Lee & the tiger cross and where Lee and the fish cross. We can also put an X where Ana and the bird cross and where Max and the bird cross.

-Clue 2 says, "Ana's favorite animal has legs and so does Lee's favorite animal."

-We already know that Lee's favorite animal likes to sit on people's shoulders.

-The only other animal that has legs is the tiger. This must be Ana's favorite.

-So, put a check mark where Ana and the tiger cross.

-That means we can put an X where Lee and the tiger cross, where Max and the tiger cross, and where Ana and the fish cross.

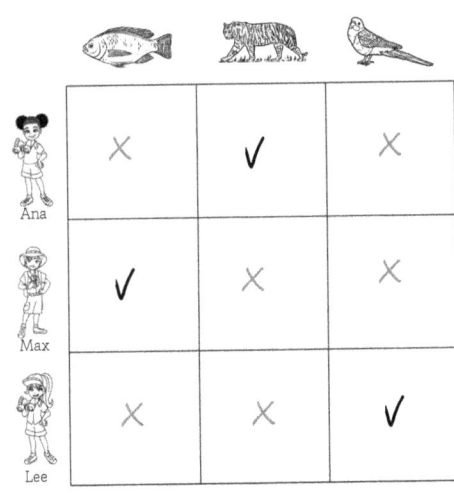

-There aren't any more clues.

-However, the only blank spot left is where Max and the fish cross.

-We know that means that the fish must be Max's favorite animal.

LOGIC MATRICES

87

HOW MANY COUNTRIES?

Ana　　　Max　　　Lee　　　Ben

	Ana	Max	Lee	Ben
2				
4				
9				
10				

Ana, Max, Lee, and Ben like to travel. They have each visited a different number of countries. How many countries has each detective visited?

Clues:

- Ana has visited 5 more than Max. (Hint: Find which numbers have a difference of 5.)
- Lee has visited less than Max.
- Max has visited less than Ana and less than Ben.

88

HOW OLD ARE THEY?

Ana   Max   Lee   Ben

	Ana	Max	Lee	Ben
8				
9				
12				
16				

Find each detective's age.

Clues:

• Ana is the youngest.

• Max's age is an odd number.

• Ben is twice as old as Ana.

WHEN DID THEY ARRIVE?

Each detective arrived to the detective agency office at a different time. Can you figure out what time each one arrived?

Clues:

- Ben arrived 1 hour before Lee. Ben arrived 1 hour after Ana.
- Ana did not arrive first.

WHAT IS THEIR FAVORITE FOOD?

Each detective has a favorite food. Can you figure out what it is?

Clues:

- Ana's food must be baked in an oven.
- Lee's food comes from a vine.   • Max's food should not be cooked.

HOW DID THEY LEAVE THE CITY?

The detectives need your help! Will you help them figure out clues about these bad guys (two men and one woman)?

Find the thing each bad guy rode in to leave the city. (They each took a different way out.)

Clues:

- The vehicle "B" used goes the fastest.
- "C" used the vehicle that never leaves the ground.

LOGIC MATRICES

WHEN DID THEY LEAVE?

Can you find out what time each bad guy left?

Clues:
- "C" left 2 hours after "A".
- "B" left after "A".

SUPER SLEUTHS CERTIFICATE

Did you do all the questions?

WRITE YOUR SCORE HERE _____

CONGRATULATIONS!

Ana   Max   Lee   Ben

WAY TO GO!

Congratulations to:

_____

(write your detective name here)

You tried your best and answered all the questions - you're now a member of the SUPER SLEUTHS!

_____
draw your
picture here

ANSWER KEY for parents and educators

NOTE: Some answer choices are not labelled A, B, C, etc. in the questions.
For these questions: Choice 1=A, Choice 2=B, Choice 3=C, Choice 4=D, Choice 5=E.

SPATIAL REASONING, P.6-27

-Picture Parts: 1-E, 2-C, 3-D, 4-B, 5-A   -Shape Groups: 1-C, 2-D, 3-B, 4-A

-Which One Does Not Belong?
1. D (4 sides)   2. E (half-filled with lines)   3. B (shapes are gray-white-gray)
4. B (small to large) 5. D (2-sided arrow)   6. A (small rectangle in the middle)
7. B (circle is in the middle of the line as the "house" rotates)
8. D (1 gray square) 9. D (2 black & 1 gray sections)   10. A (1 heart facing opposite direction/3
                                                                    hearts facing same direction)

11. C (2 kinds of shapes inside the circle's sections)   12. A (circle is next to shorter side of shape)

-What Comes Next?
2.    3.   4.

-What Is Missing?
1. C (1 shape, then 2 shapes)   2. D (shape fills with lines)
3. A (switches colors)   4. B (rotates 90 degrees)
5. C (larger & smaller shape switch)   6. C (shape gets bigger & turns black)
7. D (half of the shape)   8. C (top & middle shape switch)
9. D (shape divides into quarters; top left & bottom right become black)
10. A (shape rotatess 180 degrees & bottom becomes black)
11. D (first and second shapes switch; third and fourth shapes switch)
12. D (each half of the whole square flips)

-Puzzle Pieces
1. C   2. D   3. C   4. E

-Can You Match? p.24   1-D, 2-C, 3-A, 4-B;

                         5-H, 6-E, 7-F, 8-G

-Can You Match? p.25   1-D, 2-E, 3-A, 4-B, 5-C

-Can You Match? p.26   1-F, 2-D, 3-G, 4-A, 5-C, 6-B, 7-E;

                         1-C, 2-A, 3-E, 4-B, 5-D

ANSWER KEY for parents and educators

IDENTIFICATION, P.30-35

-Can You Find the Hidden Objects?

Lighthouse- Cape Town; Pagoda- Tokyo; Statue 1- Buenos Aires; Statue 2- Rio; Building Windows- Dubai; Tower Section- Paris; Arena Section- Rio

-Can You Spot The Difference?

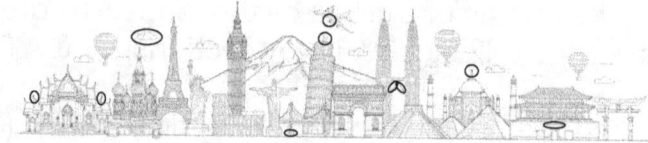

-Can You Find the Missing Piece?   1-D, 2-C, 3-L, 4-K, 5-J, 6-E, 7-H

-Can You Spot The Difference?

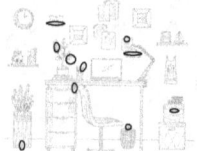
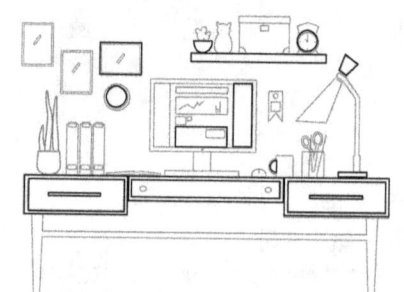

-Can You Find the Shapes? ------------------------------->

PATTERNS AND SEQUENCING, P.38-49

-What Comes Next?

1. circle	2. down arrow	3. 2 hearts	4. magnifying glass
5. magnifying glass with handle on left, lens on right			6. 2 shoeprints
7. circle	8. square with black on left & white on right		9. arrow pointing right
10. 4 down arrows	11. 5 up arrows	12. A-B-C	
13. C	14. B	15. B	16. A
17. C	18. A	19. D	20. C

-Sudoku

-p.46 :

magnifying glass	glasses	binoculars
glasses	binoculars	magnifying glass
binoculars	magnifying glass	glasses

-p.47

magnifying glass	binoculars	glasses	eye
glasses	eye	magnifying glass	binoculars
binoculars	magnifying glass	eye	glasses
eye	glasses	binoculars	magnifying glass

ANSWER KEY for parents and educators

Patterns and Sequencing, Sudoku, continued

-p.48 magnifying glass   glasses   binoculars   eye
       binoculars   eye   magnifying glass   glasses
       eye   binoculars   glasses   magnifying glass
       glasses   magnifying glass eye   binoculars

-p.49 eye   binoculars   magnifying glass   glasses
       glasses   magnifying glass binoculars   eye
       binoculars   glasses   eye   magnifying glass
       magnifying glass   eye   glasses   binoculars

VERBAL REASONING, P.52-61

-Which One Does Not Belong?
1. C (worn on head)   2. E (tell time)   3. A (cold things)
4. B (cubes)   5. B (fruit)   6. C (animal homes)
7. A (insects)   8. E (used for measurement)
9. D (carry many)   10. C (cylinders)   11. D (real animals)   12. B (pairs)

-What's Missing?
1. D (body part used with)   2. B (closed & open)   3. A (# of fingers = wheels)
4. B (older version > newer)   5. A (# of shape sides = dots)
6. C (opposites)   7. B (vehicle that travels here)   8. A (part > whole)

QUANTITATIVE REASONING, P.64-85

-Can You Balance?
1. 4, 10, 10   2. 3, 9, 18   3. 5, 7, 14   4. 6, 7, 21
5. 6, 8, 16   6. 10, 2, 4   7. 5, 10, 15   8. 8, 16, 32

-How Many Keys?   1. 6   2. 5   3. 4   4. 8   5. 8   6. 3   7. 1   8. 0

-How Many Sweets?
1. sweets: 10, 8, 12, 9; the problems: 9, 6   2. sweets: 4, 7, 19; the problem: 8

-How Much? pizza: 12, drink: 1; the problems: 12, 6, 10

-What Would You Buy? answers vary; buying everything = $370

-What's Missing?
1. D (+2)   2. C (-3)   3. D (+4)   4. A (x2)   5. D (x2 dots)
6. A (x4)   7. B (half)   8. A (x2)

ANSWER KEY for parents and educators

-Magic Squares
1. all must = 15
2. all must = 15
3. all must = 15
4. all must = 15
5. all must = 24
6. all must = 120

-What Would You Buy? p.82: buying everything = $1,810
-What Would You Buy? p.83: answers vary

LOGIC MATRICES, P.86-93

How Many Countries?

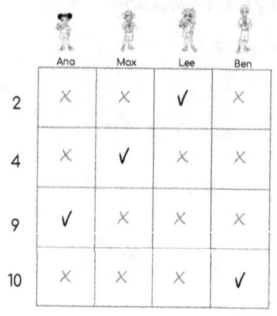

	Ana	Max	Lee	Ben
2	X	X	✓	X
4	X	✓	X	X
9	✓	X	X	X
10	X	X	X	✓

How Old Are They?

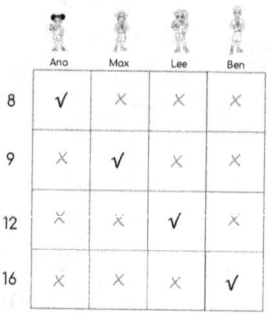

	Ana	Max	Lee	Ben
8	✓	X	X	X
9	X	✓	X	X
12	X	X	✓	X
16	X	X	X	✓

When Did They Arrive?

Ana	X	✓	X	X
Max	✓	X	X	X
Lee	X	X	X	✓
Ben	X	X	✓	X

What's Their Favorite Food?

Ana	✓	X	X	X
Max	X	✓	X	X
Lee	X	X	✓	X
Ben	X	X	X	✓

How Did They Leave the City?

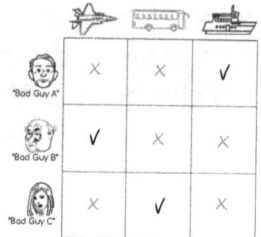

"Bad Guy A"	X	X	✓
"Bad Guy B"	✓	X	X
"Bad Guy C"	X	✓	X

When Did They Leave?

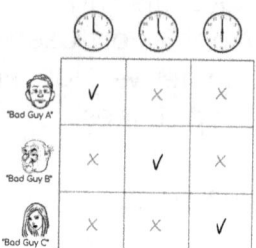

"Bad Guy A"	✓	X	X
"Bad Guy B"	X	✓	X
"Bad Guy C"	X	X	✓

For use as scratch paper, if needed.

For use as scratch paper, if needed.

www.ingramcontent.com/pod-product-compliance
Lightning Source LLC
Chambersburg PA
CBHW082110120626
46553CB00011B/3618